"Do you have a grip on what renews a parish? Most parish leaders face frustrations trying to articulate just how to help their parishes. In *Made for Mission* Glemkowski clearly lays out a practical, facts-based approach to parish revitalization and inspires a strategic focus on what really matters to me, to Real Life Catholic, and to the whole Church: the salvation offered by Jesus Christ and his mandate to make disciples. Evangelization truly is the Church's deepest identity. Get this book. Read this book. Let your leadership be transformed by this book."

— Chris Stefanick
Speaker, author, and founder of Real Life Catholic

"*Made for Mission* identifies the real crisis in the Church today as a pervasive failure to form authentic disciples. I couldn't agree more! But Tim also delivers on the practical side with tangible step-by-step guidance and tools to help you actually do it in your parish. Highly recommended!"

— Jim Beckman
Executive Director of Evangelization & Catechesis,
Archdiocese of Oklahoma City

"A bold vision for parishes is desperately needed today. Tim Glemkowski provides one that is clear, practical, and inspiring. You've got to read this book!"

— Kevin Cotter, Executive Director of The Amazing Parish

"*Made for Mission: Renewing Your Parish Culture* outlines a clear path to discipleship based on wisdom and principles that have been tested in other parishes. Tim Glemkowski weaves together a convincing case for parish renewal that is practical and accessible, sharing engaging stories and insights drawn from his work across the country. A compelling read."

— Julianne Stanz, Director of Parish Life and Evangelization, Diocese of Green Bay, Wisconsin

"*Now I can see!* Constantly bombarded with competing interests, we need someone to clearly 'paint the picture' for us, portraying both what's being communicated and our role in it. To any pastor or parish leader seeking guidance with their goals and efforts, this book is at the very top of my list of recommendations!"

— Father Matthew Wertin, Vicar for the New Evangelization, Diocese of Pueblo

"The heart of this book is a new vision for parishes, rooted in the process of evangelization. Tim makes this vision clear and practical. But it won't be easy. There's only one thing left to change the future of our parishes: pastors and their staff embracing this challenging vision."

— Edmund Mitchell, Director of Evangelization and Catechesis, St. Francis of Assisi Catholic Church, Grapevine, Texas

Made for Mission
Renewing Your Parish Culture

MADE FOR
MISSION

RENEWING YOUR
PARISH CULTURE

TIM GLEMKOWSKI

Our Sunday Visitor
Huntington, Indiana

Nihil Obstat
Msgr. Michael Heintz, Ph.D.
Censor Librorum

Imprimatur
✠ Kevin C. Rhoades
Bishop of Fort Wayne-South Bend
July 15, 2019

Our Sunday Visitor Publishing Division
Our Sunday Visitor, Inc.
200 Noll Plaza
Huntington, IN 46750
1-800-348-2440

ISBN: 978-1-68192-458-8 (Inventory No. T2344)
1. RELIGION—Christianity—Catholic. 2. RELIGION—Christian Ministry—General. 3. RELIGION—Christian Ministry—Pastoral Resources.

eISBN: 978-1-68192-459-5
LCCN: 2019946662

Cover and interior design: Lindsey Riesen
Cover art: Shutterstock.com

PRINTED IN THE UNITED STATES OF AMERICA

DEDICATION

This book, L'Alto Catholic Institute, and my own relationship with God would not exist without the prayer, selfless love, and support of so many. To those who have journeyed with me in this work, I express my deepest gratitude and dedicate this book.

To my parents, Jim and Debbie Glemkowski, for always believing that God has more.

To my siblings, Jill, Steve, Christie, Dan, Joe, Rene, Tom, and Clare, for your friendship.

To Monsignor Dan Deutsch, whose patience and witness have been a constant guide throughout the years.

To Elliot and Jessica Foley, for over a decade of friendship that has taught me about what God's heart is actually like.

To Michael and Emily Bianco, who came up with the idea for L'Alto on Mount Falcon Trail years ago and for your steadfast support ever since.

To Mark and Laurel Balasa, whose generosity and counsel have made the dream of L'Alto Catholic Institute a reality.

To Deacon Keith Strohm, for his mentorship and for believing in L'Alto when it was still just a website.

To my children, Eva, Theo, and Elizabeth, who are my life's greatest joy.

Finally, and always, to my wife, Magdalene.

God has created me to do Him some definite service;
He has committed some work to me
which He has not committed to another.
I have my mission —

He has not created me for naught.
I shall do good;
I shall do His work;
I shall be an angel of peace,
a preacher of truth in my own place, while not intend-
ing it,
if I do but keep His Commandments.

... Therefore I will trust Him.

— Cardinal John Henry Newman

CONTENTS

CONTENTS

AUTHOR'S NOTE

I wrote this book for you, the parish leader, influencer, staff member, priest, or pastor. There is an old Chinese curse, "May he live in interesting times." It is no secret that we live in difficult and interesting times for our world and in our Church, but it is no accident that God has chosen us for these times. No matter our frailties and weaknesses, our sinfulness and worries, God has put us in this place for a reason, and he has committed to us some definite good to do. Somehow, in some way, we are called to be a part of the renewal of the Church that is so desperately needed, both for the sake of our members and those who are still outside the Church.

I hope that you find this book to be a benefit and a support in your labors. Please know of my prayers for you, that God will make you the great saint he has called you to be, that he will bless your efforts to renew your parish's culture, and that he will bring many others to himself through your efforts.

God bless you.

FOREWORD

I'm a science fiction nerd. (Bear with me, this will be relevant in just a few sentences.)

That's why one of my favorite quotes from any movie comes from the title character of the 1984 cult-classic movie, *The Adventures of Buckaroo Banzai Across the 8th Dimension*. In a moment of intentional profundity, Buckaroo lays down the following wisdom: "No matter where you go, there you are."

It's an axiom that is so self-evident it almost acts as a caricature — and yet it has stuck with me through all these years as a reminder to be present to whatever geographical, social, cultural, or historical context in which I find myself.

That's a lesson the Church needs to learn today.

The Church currently occupies a particularly fraught and changing sociocultural space in the twenty-first century. Books like *Forming Intentional Disciples* and sociological studies from Gallup and the Pew Research Center have brought these realities to our attention, but more urgently, we are living them out in parishes all across North America and Europe.

Certainly, the news isn't all doom and gloom. Life in the twenty-first century — with global instability, the breakdown of former superpowers, and a growing persecution of Christians across the globe — is more like life in the early Church, which was one of the greatest and most accelerated periods of Church growth not fueled simply by "birthing" new Catholics. Post-modernity, while resistant to truth claims, has a particular heart for stories, and we believe in a God who has invited us into his very story — the story of an unending and triumphant love.

In such a time as this, the last thing the Church needs is another program, another canned response, or a structural process that purports to do the hard work of accompaniment and disciple-making. The crisis the Church faces today *is* one of discipleship, and that crisis extends to almost every layer of leadership in the Church. Discipleship and evangelization cannot be understood from the outside. Without a personal relationship with Christ and practical experience in helping others encounter Christ, walking with them into relationship with him, forming them as mature disciples, and equipping them as missionary focused men and women eager to share Christ with others, parish and diocesan leaders will be unable to create cultures and structures that support evangelization and mission. In short, they will be unable to bear the particular fruit that Jesus expects.

That's what excites me so much about this book.

Tim Glemkowski is a personal friend and a colleague. He is passionate, knowledgeable, and articulate. But more importantly, he possesses the kind of experience that Church leaders need today. *Made for Mission* breaks open the hard-won wisdom Tim has gained by laboring in the trenches and "doing" the work of renewal alongside dozens of parishes. In this book, he presents a very Christ-centered approach to cultural change and parish transformation.

But be warned.

What you have before you is not a silver bullet, or a detailed playbook that you can use to check off the right steps and simply glide into the new reality of your parish. Rather, it is a masterclass in the application of critical principles through which our parishes, in cooperation with the grace of God, can truly be transformed.

The hard work — the blood, sweat, and tears — are all

yours.

This book, however, provides a clear path.

In my work with almost a hundred parishes and dioceses over the last twenty years in the area of parish transformation and renewal, I would have been blessed beyond measure to possess a resource like this.

God bless you as you dive into its pages and continue on your journey of parish renewal.

Deacon Keith Strohm
Author of *Ablaze: 5 Essential Paradigm Shifts*
for Parish Renewal
Executive Director, M3 Ministries

CHAPTER 1

Changing Culture in a Changing Culture

The very last Blockbuster video store in the United States can be found in the town of Bend, Oregon.[1] The franchisee who proudly operates this last bastion of a key 1990s cultural touchpoint said in an interview: "It's very nostalgic. We have a bunch of 19-year-olds working here; it's fun explaining to them what a floppy disk was."[2]

Personally, it is strange for me to believe that a Blockbuster store can already be considered "nostalgic." I do not feel old enough to have such vivid memories of something that is now of a past era. Nothing defined my middle school years more than riding my bike down to our local Blockbuster store to rent the latest video game (I found that a five day rental period was enough time to finish a game … if you didn't eat or sleep) or a Chris Farley movie.

The glory of Blockbuster was in the experience of visiting the store itself. People would spend twenty minutes combing through the various aisles looking for a movie, finally whittling their decision down to one or two options before just taking the plunge. Often, the movie you came in to rent was not the one you ended up getting because you stumbled on an old favorite or saw that fresh-out-of-theaters title you had been meaning to see. Then, as you reached the counter, you found yourself surrounded on either side by aisles of candy and popcorn, a perfect complement to your movie-watching experience.

Blockbuster eventually crashed up against the stark reality of the convenience of Netflix, founded in 1997. How could Blockbuster compete with a flat fee, unlimited rentals from the comfort of your own home, and no late fees? Netflix began to boom as DVD players became cheaper, starting around 2002. By the time Netflix began streaming movies on-demand on its online platform in 2007, whether Blockbuster knew it or not, it was dead in the water.

As Blockbuster's death spiral began, they tried to copy Netflix in an effort to compete with them. First, they introduced their own DVD mailing businesses. My family, as loyal Blockbuster customers, switched from Netflix to their mailing service for a while. They even tried out some online streaming of their own. Nothing worked. By 2013, all corporate-owned Blockbuster stores were shuttered, and the DVD-mailing business was closed down. Why did nothing work?

Experts disagree on why exactly Blockbuster's attempts to compete with Netflix did not save its business. I think it comes down to one thing: Netflix had a vision and Blockbuster did not. Netflix understood that the entire culture was fundamentally changing. They launched their streaming service in the same year that Apple announced the iPhone.[3] Both Netflix and Apple knew that just tweaking their business model was not enough; they had to understand the cultural moment and propose simple and bold solutions that could meet that moment head-on. Blockbuster, weighed down under so much infrastructure from building a business for a different era, was not agile enough to compete. Instead of responding boldly with new initiatives that would inspire the marketplace, Blockbuster reacted defensively and ended up just slowing their decline.

What does this have to do with the Catholic Church and

our parishes specifically? It provides a cautionary tale as we discern the best way to tackle the current situation of decline in many of our parishes. It is no secret that the Catholic Church in the West today is hemorrhaging members. Most of us have heard some the dire statistics, but it helps to look briefly at the current situation and the numbers.

From 2007 to 2014, the share of Americans who identify as Catholic dropped from 24 percent to 21 percent. Of those who still identify as Catholic, 35 percent belong to the "Baby Boomer" generation (born between 1944 and 1964), while only 22 percent are Millennials — currently the largest generation in the United States.[4] This means that the dire condition of many Catholic parishes will only worsen over the next couple of decades, if nothing changes. This is why it seems that every few months we hear of new parish closings in what were formerly bastions of Catholic life and culture.[5] According to CARA (Center for Applied Research in the Apostolate), which is affiliated with Georgetown University, the number of parishes in the United States peaked in 1990 at 19,620 parishes. By 2018, even with parishes continuing to open in certain parts of the country, that number was down to 17,007.[6]

Granted, there are still many committed, faithful Catholics who love the Church and continue to be active members of their local parish, and signs for hope exist across the country. Yet too many Catholics are simply walking away.

Our cultural moment is changing, and it is becoming increasingly apparent that we are entering into a secularizing age. With respect to this secularization, the United States just passed a critical threshold this year, with the "nones," or those who claim no religious affiliation at all, surpassing Catholics and evangelicals as the largest religious group in the United States.[7] In the early to mid-1970s, only about 5 percent of the U.S. population called themselves "nones." By 1995, that number was still just below 10 percent. In the last twenty-five years, the number has shot up to over 23 percent in the United States.

In a country of around 325 million people, that means about 75 million of them no longer claim a religious affiliation. We are living in an era of *rapid* secularization and cultural change, unlike anything this part of the world has ever seen. For the Church, this means that renewal — both at the highest level and in every parish — is not just a nice idea; it is imperative. What we need is a new apostolic age.

With my apostolate, L'Alto Catholic Institute (laltocatholic.com), I have worked personally with dozens of parishes who are seeing these discouraging trends played out in real time. The leaders in these parishes recognize that their membership is declining and aging but feel overwhelmed and at a loss for what they can actually do about the problem. This on-the-ground experience has proved to me that, given the macro changes that are taking place culturally, parishes can no longer view themselves as gathering places for the faithful. Rather, they must see themselves as missionary outposts in a new and strange land. We, as a Church and as parishes, no longer operate in a Christian culture. In this post-Christian moment, we are called to be radically on mission.

> *Parishes can no longer view themselves as gathering places for the faithful. Rather, they must see themselves as missionary outposts in a new and strange land.*

Working with parishes, I have become convicted that while the increased conversation around parish renewal happening in the professional Church world today is encouraging, a greater emphasis on helping parishes change *their* culture to meet *the* culture head-on needs to be diffused more widely. The result is this book.

To put it plainly, I have personally seen too many parishes trying to stem the tide of declining membership by simply tweaking tactics. Too often, unsure of what else to do, parishes seek to fix a much deeper problem with surface-level solutions. "Let's try a new program! A different curriculum! That new

Bible study! A few more greeters at Mass! A new mission statement!" The problem is that none of these solutions addresses the core problem. When parishes focus their renewal efforts around things like "engagement," they are putting Band-Aids on a much deeper wound.

It is up to us to ensure that the Church does not respond to this cultural moment like Blockbuster, by just chasing the trends, always a step behind, desperately hoping to cling to some of her membership and manage decline. My hope is that the Church takes this difficult cultural moment and uses it to boldly lean in to her perennial vocation: to be on mission to save souls.

This is what Pope Saint John Paul II called for when he proclaimed the New Evangelization. This phrase "new evangelization" has come to mean all kinds of things in the Church, including in some contexts especially the use of new media in sharing the Gospel. Yet John Paul was calling for more than that. He was inviting the Church to dramatically reorient herself in the present age, given the cultural trends. Prophetically aware of the challenges already facing the Church and those to come, this great pope proclaimed that he saw "the dawning of a new missionary age, which will become a radiant day bearing an abundant harvest, if all Christians ... respond with generosity ... to the calls and challenges of our times."[8]

THE CRUCIAL ROLE OF THE PARISH

The parish is the Church's great missionary opportunity. Think about it: All of our "church planting" has already been done! We have outposts of Catholic faithful set up throughout the world, ready to encounter the broader community and culture in which they are placed. Yet too often, especially in the United States, the parish experience is not mission-focused at all. For many Catholics in the United States, the parish experience could be summed up in one word: comfortable. The familiar culture of far too many parishes involves polite suburban people gathering together socially on Sunday mornings and mumbling their way through common prayers before returning to the "real world." We are seeing the results of this culture all too clearly.

To understand how we got here and what we can do about it, it helps to look more closely at what a parish is, and what it is supposed to be. Did you know that the parish itself is not a building but an area of land? They still call counties "parishes" in the state of Louisiana, a traditionally Catholic area, and this is itself instructive. When we are talking about a parish, we are not referring only to a building owned by the Catholic Church and the Catholics who choose to become members, we are also referring to a geographic region.

Over the centuries, the Church has divided up the entire world into these parishes. By doing so, she has planted outposts of her mission in local communities around the world. Each parish is a local instantiation of the universal Body of Christ. The reason for this is not just to have a place for Catholics to gather, but to show the community of Catholics in any particular area the extent of their shared mission field. Within a given parish's boundaries, the priests' job is to sanctify the baptized faithful. The baptized faithful also have a job within those parish boundaries: to sanctify one another within the Body of Christ, and to reach out to those not in full communion with the Church. It is that simple.

For the vast majority of Catholics, almost their entire experience of the Faith will be mediated through the parish. Yet too many of our parishes are clinging to ways of functioning that could not be more out of touch with the presently demanded apostolic moment. So many of our modalities of functioning have been crafted for a cultural moment that no longer exists, one that was much more supportive of religious practice in the wider culture. Even if it does not reach the fullness of the parish's mission, maintenance of the parish structures is all that a Christian cultural context requires to keep the doors open.

Though this shift has been happening for hundreds of years, the second half of the twentieth century saw this cultural revolution toward a post-Christian society fully mature. We now operate as a Church in what is called a "post-Christian society." The Christian worldview and praxis are no longer the dominant forms of life in Europe and North America. Traditional morality and religious belief are seen, not just as optional, but as outdated and even repugnant.

Art and entertainment tend to reflect the underlying culture. To take one stark example, consider the Colosseum and the pagan culture of ancient Rome, which it represents. Then consider our own entertainment culture today. In 1953, a Catholic bishop standing in front of a blackboard talking about the moral issues of the day pulled in ten million viewers a week and won the Emmy for "Most Outstanding Television Personality."[9] In 2018–19, the runaway top TV show among adults 18 to 49, *Game of Thrones,* frequently featured graphic nudity, extreme violence, and various forms of assault. When John Lennon famously remarked in a 1966 interview that the Beatles were "more popular than Jesus"[10] and that rock 'n roll would outlive Christianity, maybe he was not only being arrogant, but pointing to a seismic shift in culture that was already taking place.

In our post-Christian society, there has been a rapid and significant breakdown in the family. This is an issue for parishes because we have based many of our parish realities on the strength of the domestic church. As a Church, we have relied on the family unit to support and sustain most of our initiatives. In an ideal world, the parish in all of its structures would exist to support the strong formation that is already taking place at home. In reality, the sacramental numbers alone testify to a weakening of the domestic church in our parishes. While there were 420,000 Catholic marriages in 1970, in 2018 that number dwindled to a generational low of 143,000.

It should be no surprise, then, that while there were almost 1.1 million infant baptisms in 1970, in 2018 that number was 615,000.[11]

When the overall culture supports religious practice, churches get to do ministry as if it is "bumper bowling." As long as we throw the ball toward the pins, it is going to get there. We may not have a strike every time, but we will at least hit a couple of pins by default! In our current day, the bumpers have been taken off completely. There are almost no cultural pressures to guide current or future generations back into the Church. On the contrary, increasing social pressures are drawing people — including many baptized Catholics — away from the Church Jesus founded.

Clearly, we live today in a very different cultural moment, but many of our parishes are still operating in a "maintenance" mode that would only make sense in a Christian cultural context. In the face of this mounting secularizing shift, many parishes in the United States and other parts of the world are simply not structured to turn things around.

It is crucial that we understand the challenge that now faces our parishes. If we consider our problems to be temporal and shallow, then we might be tempted to think that simply tweaking things will produce the desired results of a renewed Church. Yet maintenance solutions alone cannot turn things around. Only a radical recommitment to our Church's missionary identity is a fitting response to the revolution taking place in the world. Too often in parishes, we are "playing not to lose" rather than "playing to win." Today, more is required. What is needed to meet the challenges today's parishes face is not just a more effective form of maintenance, but a complete transformation into continually operating on mission, like the first apostles who burst out of the Upper Room on Pentecost.

Until now, to make a broad generalization, the New Evangelization that Pope Saint John Paul II called for has been carried out largely in ecclesial movements and ministries. We have not done enough in our parishes, and thankfully, we are beginning to make this a priority. We must figure out how to transform these communities whose structures are often built only for maintenance, and re-purpose them for mission. If we do not, we will miss our key advantage for re-Christifying our postmodern world. In the end, the fulfillment of the call to the New Evangelization will depend on the parish, because the parish is the place where salvation history and people's individual lives meet.

The fulfillment of the call to the New Evangelization will depend on the parish, because the parish is the place where salvation history and people's individual lives meet.

This means that in order to renew the whole Church, we have to first renew the parish.

That is the whole point of this book. My full-time work for many years has been to accompany parishes through a process of renewal focused on discipleship. Through that work, and by encountering parishes of all sizes, I have learned a few key principles about what works and what does not.

Each parish is unique, with a rich history and pastoral context that changes the tactics that might work at ground-level. A "one-size-fits-all" approach to parish renewal simply cannot work, and there is no quick and easy process for renewing a parish, so this book will not seek to propose one. What it does propose is a map of sorts for long-term cultural change. I am convinced that, if each parish takes seriously the challenges of this moment, and proactively works to meet them head-on, the new missionary age prophesied by Saint John Paul II will come about. To me, creating this kind of momentum requires that parish leaders focus singularly on four simple keys, which we will discuss in more detail in a moment.

It is incredibly important that these keys be simple. Parish leaders today are often discouraged and overwhelmed. They have been trying to do well and to effect change for so long, with so much resistance and inertia, that they are burned out. They feel overworked and underappreciated. Many feel cynical about the possibility that their parish culture can ever really change. The to-do list is already full and the thought of trying to drive such change feels like a thousand new tasks that they just do not have the time or energy for.

If this is your situation, I come bearing good news. Parish renewal is not about running off in a thousand directions like chickens with our heads cut off. This scattershot approach to renewal leaves parishes disorganized and parish leadership burned out. My vision for parish renewal involves, not multiplying our efforts and doing more, but doing *less*. And who doesn't love doing less?

Really, renewing a parish and creating a culture of missionary discipleship is about doing less because it is about prioritizing a few things and doing them really, really well.

Take a secular example. In-N-Out Burger, a fast food restaurant chain found in the western part of the United States, particularly California, has long had an almost mythical relationship with its loyal customers. In-N-Out does not have the huge menu of a McDonalds, but lines are out the door at all times of the day. Recently, one Los Angeles newspaper referred to their drive-thru lines as a "public menace" due to their length.[12] Their secret? They do a few things incredibly well using fresh ingredients. They focus on a small number of food items, but everything they do is top quality. Because they have a smaller menu, they have the ability to be intentional and expert in everything they attempt.

Now consider your parish. Each parish is unique, so it is difficult to propose a top-down, one-size-fits-all model for parish renewal. However, through personal experience, through analyzing the very best missional parishes, and through pulling from the magisterial teachings of the Church, we can come to some definite principles that can be universally applied to any parish situation to begin the movement from maintenance to mission.

To effect such a change will not be the work of a moment, or even a year or two, but will be the work of the next ten years. We need to begin with this big-picture vision of a complete cultural overhaul, from focusing inward on maintenance to moving outward toward mission and forming disciples. Only a goal that big will inspire the work that will be required.

Below are four strategic goals that can focus your efforts and break down the massive project of parish renewal into more achievable steps. I call these the four keys to parish renewal, as they lay out, not a step-by-step, one-size-fits-all path for any parish, but the four main drivers that inspire and propel our efforts to renew the culture in our parishes. As we seek to build our parishes into missionary outposts of the New Evangelization, these four keys help us determine simple and actionable ways we get there.

They are as follows:

1) The vision is clear. We want ours to be a missional parish aimed at introducing parishioners and non-parishioners alike to a life-changing relationship with Jesus Christ.

2) There is a clear path to discipleship. We want our parish to be equipped and formed to help people grow into the fullness of mature Catholicism and missionary discipleship.

3) Leaders are well-formed, empowered, and sent to bear fruit. We want our parish to form leaders who are fruitful both within the parish and in the larger community in their day-to-day lives.

4) Nothing in the parish operates in maintenance mode. We want everything our parish does to be aligned with the mission to form disciples who can make disciples.

This book is written to guide you through these four keys to parish renewal and give you practical strategies for implementing them. With the conviction that the renewal of the Church depends on the renewal of the parish, and the renewal of the parish depends on forming missionary disciples, we will be unpacking these four keys to show you how to move your parish from a culture of maintaining decline to one that is radically on mission and forming missionary disciples.

While the "meat" of this book will focus on how to implement these four keys in your parish context (chapters 4–8), we first have to pause to lay some groundwork. Before we throw up the walls of the house, we have to lay the foundation. Like we said earlier, unless we properly diagnose the problem, we will not know what the right remedies are or how to contextualize them appropriately in our parish. So first, we will look at the four types of parishes in the United States and take a moment to diagnose where your parish may be. Second, we will propose the antidote and this book's overall vision for cultural change: forming missionary disciples.

TWO IMPORTANT NOTES ON RENEWAL

Before we move on, I also want to stress what we mean by "renewal." There are two important things to note as you read this book and consider renewal in your own parish.

First: Renewal is not something we do.

Jesus is abundantly clear about this: "Apart from me, you can do nothing" (Jn 15:5).

As we are going to talk about, real parish renewal depends on changed lives and new disciples. You and I do not have the power on our own to form a single disciple. At the end of the day, it is God alone who makes this happen through his grace.

The power of the Holy Spirit brings about renewal. We cooperate through what we do, but we cannot do it alone.

If we believed that truth more fully as a Church, we would pray and act differently, and we would start to see real change. If I could point to a single reason why we have not seen more wide-scale renewal in our parishes, it is because we as leaders do not really believe that God is

The best way to start renewal: Pray consistently, intentionally, over time, with others for God to bring about change.

fully in control. The best way to start renewal: pray consistently, intentionally, over time, with others for God to bring about change. We have to actually believe and act like it is God alone who can do the work that is required. Plans are great; prayers are better. We need both for renewal to happen.

Saint John of the Cross puts it better than I can:

> Let those then who are singularly active, who think they can win the world with their preaching and exterior works, observe here that they would profit the Church and please God much more ... were they to spend at least half of this time with God in prayer. ... They would then certainly accomplish more, and with less labor, by one work than they otherwise would by a thousand. ... Without prayer they would do a great deal of hammering but accomplish little, and sometimes nothing, and even at times cause harm. ... However much they may appear to achieve externally, they will in substance be accomplishing nothing [without a deep life of prayer].[13]

You are our only hope, Lord.

Second: Authentic renewal is always authentically Catholic.

Many faithful Catholics in our time are wary of the concept of "renewal." This is not without reason. Too many watched as the excited language about renewal following the Second Vatican Council amounted to little more than watering down the Faith and adapting to modernity. Often this left the Church looking more like the world, and it did not help the Church reach and transform the world as she is called to do. Rather than authentic renewal, the reforms following the council often looked more like revolution.

This is not what I am proposing. What I do propose is in line with the helpful hermeneutic for renewal George Weigel provides in his book, *Evangelical Catholicism*. He claims that authentic renewal always asks of each reality, first, "What is the truth of this thing?" Authentic renewal should never fundamentally change the objective reality of any teachings or practices of the Faith. At the same time, authentic renewal also asks, "How can this best be approached in light of mission?"[14] *Both* of these questions need to be posed to all that we do in our parishes as we seek renewal. Authentic renewal will pull from our rich heritage as Catholics and will change nothing about the deposit of faith, but it will be bold in prioritizing mission. Authentic renewal is not just about changing the Church, it is about unleashing the Gospel.

It is the aim of this book to pose those questions with you and seek out answers together. Drawn from the experience of working with real parishes, with an acute eye and respect for the differences in the pastoral situations found within each community, we will try to propose some solutions for those of you who want to embark on cultural change in your parish but are still looking for more meat on the bones in terms of how. The purpose of this book is not just to convince you that cultural change is necessary. This is for anyone who is aware of the present difficulties in carrying forward the Church's mission, and who wants to start wrestling with how we are going to focus our parishes on mission.

CHAPTER 2

Diagnosing Your Parish

In our work at L'Alto Catholic Institute, coaching dozens of parishes on disciple-making initiatives, we have come to realize that parishes in the United States today generally fit into one of four broad categories. Outlining these four types of parishes has proven to be a helpful diagnostic tool, especially for parish leaders who might have trouble convincing the rest of the parish leadership that renewal is what is required.

I am convinced that the renewal of the Church is not a ridiculous pipe dream, but is really God's own dream and desire for his Church. That is the destination. However, to get there, just like when we use Google Maps to get somewhere, we first have to know our current location. On the phone, that's easy enough: there is a built-in tracking device to show where you are starting from. For parishes, unfortunately, it is not so easy. We may have a general sense of where we are at as a parish, but not everyone might be in agreement. We have tried to lay out the destination already: a parish renewed around a vision for mission. But how do we describe where we are? Hopefully, you will find the tool below helpful for determining your current situation as a parish.

THE FOUR TYPES OF PARISHES

To help you diagnose your own parish's situation, I have outlined four basic possibilities when it comes to parish health, especially within the United States. They are the:

1) Dying Parish
2) Declining Parish
3) Swelling Parish
4) Growing (Healthy) Parish

Dying

Dying parishes are on their last legs. An example is my dad's childhood parish on the South Side of Chicago, once the largest archdiocese in the United States, now undergoing a process to close dozens of parishes and schools over the next few years.[15] When my dad was growing up, there were three Catholic parishes within a few blocks of each other. Each parochial school was packed; my dad remembers being in a classroom of sixty kids taught by one overwhelmed religious sister. This was a Polish neighborhood, and eventually kids grew up and moved out. The newcomers who replaced them were not always Catholic. At a certain point, dad's parish hit a tipping point: There were not enough Catholics left to sustain a community there. This is a harsh reality faced by many parishes today.

Generally speaking, most dying parishes are in urban centers in post-Christian cities. Once, huge Catholic populations required massive infrastructure to support them. Many dioceses decided to build clusters of smaller parishes that served each different ethnic group as Catholic immigrants poured into these cities. This booming population of Catholics has not been present for a generation or more, so we are starting to see a lot of the dioceses and archdioceses with many of these dying parishes close them down to consolidate resources. This can often lead to confusion and heartbreak. If done correctly, however, this can be a catalyst for mission. Some of these communities have reached a certain point where revitalization becomes difficult, if not impossible. As painful as it is, the best option may be for a dying parish to combine with other communities to create a solid base from which to bring renewal.

My challenge to you if you currently minister in or attend a dying parish is this: Focus on what you can control and not what you cannot. You likely are not in charge of whether your parish doors will close in the next decade or so. You *are* in charge of what you do with the mission territory that God has given to you.

People in your community still need to hear the Gospel preached. Pray for the Holy Spirit to inspire renewal in your neighborhood, and get creative. Instead of giving in to discouragement about your dwindling numbers, go find the people where they are and love them. The Gospel is never irrelevant, and God can still work miracles through your efforts if you let him. Do not worry about huge outreaches; reach out to individual souls and bring them to Jesus. While you are in your area, you can love the neighbors around you, even if it is just one at a time.

Instead of giving in to discouragement about your dwindling numbers, go find the people where they are and love them.

Declining

Most parishes in the United States today are declining, whether they realize it or not. This reality might sound scary, and it should. Yet the even scarier thing about declining parishes is that often the decline is hidden. Many declining parishes still actually appear to be pretty healthy. In many cases, overall attendance has stayed about the same for the last generation or so, the weekly offertory is still about where it was twenty years ago, and everything appears to be relatively stable. Yet underneath the surface, there are cracks. While it appears to be healthy, in reality this parish is simply in maintenance mode, and we know by now (from the statistics noted in the first chapter on the rise of the nones, fallen-away Catholics, and religious practice in younger generations), maintenance mode is itself decline.

Here is the harsh reality: In our current context, many parishes today might seem like healthy, vibrant churches that are maintaining things just fine, but they are actually declining parishes. The parish that you attend that is relatively full on Sundays, has a decent school, and is fairly busy with ministries and activities, is actually declining. Here is what I mean by that.

Though the facade of health remains, and the parish might even have a lot of ministries, declining parishes are not driven to form disciples. This means that this parish will hit a demographic cliff in twenty years, when the core of the parish is no longer around, if something does not change. How can you tell if your parish is merely in maintenance mode? Take a look at these other areas of your parish life. Religious education classes are much smaller than they were twenty years ago. There are fewer young families in the pews, leading to a higher average age. Fewer people are engaged in the life of the parish.

These parishes need to commit to revitalization today before they hit a point where it will become much more difficult. Thankfully, the people and the resources are still there to drive renewal, if your parish is willing to commit to doing the hard work. You, the parish leader in the declining parish, have this difficult conundrum in front of you. Your parish is at a crossroads.

Swelling

There are some parishes, typically in areas where there has been huge population growth over a short period of time, that are currently swelling. In some areas, the suburban sprawl reached what used to be a more rural community and new developments have led to a huge influx of families and not enough parishes to support them all. Some of these parishes have 5,000 families or more. The danger here is that the growth in numbers can be mistaken for health or even "success" in terms of the mission of the Church. Activity can be seen as vitality. These parishes must scratch beneath the surface to see if they are really accomplishing the Church's mission of forming disciples.

Just because attendance and offertory are up does not mean the parish is fulfilling its mission. Sometimes, if you look at the numbers, the parish is not growing at the same rate as the surrounding area.

If your parish is swelling, then you have been greatly blessed by your circumstances! Try to avoid the temptation to rest on your laurels. Do not let growth in numbers become a substitute for growth in discipleship, which is the reason behind your parish's existence. Too many parishes that are dwindling now bought into the idea years ago that maintenance mode was an okay thing because people kept showing up. You do not have some of the immediate pressures other parishes might be experiencing that make them feel the drive to revitalization, but pray that the Lord sends you a sense of urgency for mission, nonetheless. At the end of the day, our job at parishes is to bring every soul in our parish boundary into a living relationship with Jesus Christ in his Church, not just to have people show up.

Growing

There is one (and only one) true diagnostic marker of a growing and healthy parish: It is forming disciples. These parishes feel different. The adoration chapel is full. Confession lines are full. The parish has dynamic outreach to the community both in terms of social justice and evangelization. Members of the parish are living out the mission of spreading the Gospel in their own lives. A growing parish sees reasonable growth

There is one (and only one) true diagnostic marker of a growing and healthy parish: It is forming disciples.

in numbers and donations, and it is replicating across multiple generations. Even if the parish is in an area seeing demographic decline, the numbers of families in the parish is actually holding steady or even growing. Dozens are baptized at the Easter Vigil every year, and people are having life-changing encounters with Jesus on a regular basis. This is the parish you want to be, and it is the parish Jesus wants you to be.

Growing parishes might not yet be all the way to full renewal as a missionary outpost of the New Evangelization, but they are at least on the way there, and they have committed to the long-term journey of bringing about renewal by forming disciples.

HOW DO WE BECOME A GROWING, HEALTHY PARISH?

Which of the above four types of parishes is yours?

While the dying parishes are a sad part of our Church's story right now in the United States, the real danger is the declining and swelling parishes. The temptation for these parishes is to stay in maintenance mode, because at least no one is trying to close the doors of their parish. People are still coming for now, and we have enough to stay open.

It could be said that the key deadly sin to pray against in these churches is sloth. Sloth, according to Saint Thomas Aquinas, is "sorrow for spiritual good." Our parishes are being called to a great spiritual good right now: mission. Will we have the courage and conviction to follow through?

A parish can never be content to stand still. If a parish does not become missional, it will inevitably begin to decline. Growing and swelling parishes eventually become declining parishes if they lose their focus on their true calling. And declining parishes eventually become dying parishes if they do not seek to turn the trend around. We have already seen this happen in many communities over the last few generations.

Here are the two basic hallmarks of a healthy, growing parish:

1) Everyone in the parish understands that the mission of the parish is to form disciples both of those in the pews and outside her walls.
2) Everyone has an abundantly clear understanding of how that happens in the parish and in their own lives using their unique gifts.

Being a healthy parish is about actually making these principles a reality in your parish. Growing parishes know that their mission as a parish is to form disciples. They have a clear understanding of how that happens, and they have been faithfully carrying out that mission for a decade, leading to culture change over time. Everything else — the programs you use, different outreaches, events, groups — is just tactics. Whatever tactics you use, you are learning how to imbue those two principles in everything you do as a parish.

That is it. It is that simple. But of course, "simple" does not mean easy, and becoming a healthy parish is not going to be easy. First and foremost, it requires that you adopt Christ's own vision for the parish as your own. You must make the mission to form disciples central to everything that happens, but the mission cannot be just a statement on a website. It must also involve a strategic plan to get there. To create such a plan for our parishes, we need first of all to have a clear understanding of the current crisis in our Church. In the next chapter, we will look at the real crisis and how we as a Church can and should be addressing it.

SELF-DIAGNOSIS

Here is a simple quiz to help you see whether or not your parish is a "growing" parish. For each question, answer either (1) Strongly Disagree, (2) Somewhat Disagree, (3) Neutral, (4) Somewhat Agree, or (5) Strongly Agree.

1) Our parish has a shared vision and/or mission statement that focuses on the importance of discipleship for our community.

    1   2   3   4   5

2) The vast majority of our regular parish community knows what our vision and/or mission as a parish is.

    1   2   3   4   5

3) Our pastor has a leadership team that supports him in discipleship and evangelization efforts at a strategic level.

    1   2   3   4   5

4) Our homilists regularly preach on the need for a relationship with Jesus.

    1   2   3   4   5

5) Our parish has staff members available specifically for the work of evangelization and discipleship.

    1   2   3   4   5

6) Our parish has evangelization opportunities readily available to everyone in our community.

   1   2   3   4   5

7) Our parish has discipleship opportunities readily available to everyone in our community.

   1   2   3   4   5

8) The vast majority of our parish community understands what it means to be a disciple of Jesus.

   1   2   3   4   5

9) The vast majority of our parish community has attended an evangelization series and/or been a part of a discipleship small group.

   1   2   3   4   5

10) Parishioners are encouraged to become leaders and provided with formation and training to do so multiple times a year.

   1   2   3   4   5

Add up your totals. A score of 50 indicates a strong, growing parish, which is what we all want to be. A lower score shows that improvement is needed in certain areas if we want to become a strong, growing parish.

Every parish in the United States should be able to strongly agree to all 10 points in the self-diagnosis. These should just be simple hallmarks of any church that wants to form disciples. While this is not a "letter grade," growing parishes will have scores well into the 40s. The goal of this book is to give you some simple tools so that in five years, you can answer "Strongly Agree" to all of the above. Before we can explore these tools, however, we need to look at the real crisis at hand, namely, the crisis of discipleship in our parishes. In the next chapter, we will take an in-depth look at this crisis to give you the information you need to turn your parish into a growing, healthy parish.

CHAPTER 3

Addressing the Real Crisis

The real crisis in the Church is not the priest shortage, dipping donations, or even the low percentage of Catholics who attend Sunday Mass. These are just symptoms of a deeper cultural problem. The crisis in the Church is our pervasive failure over multiple generations to form disciples.

What our parishes need is not just a few new ways of doing things; they need a complete overhaul of culture. That word, "culture," is the sum total of the unspoken values, attitudes, biases, and behavioral norms of a group. It is the lens through which that group interprets reality, yet it remains largely unspoken. The culture of a parish is often felt long before it is understood or articulated. Whether we are aware of it or not, any visitor or newcomer to our community begins to feel the culture of the place before we have a chance to say a single thing about who we are and who we want to be.

Consider a positive example. Christ the King parish in Ann Arbor, Michigan, has long been known (to those who know of it) as one of the most vibrant parishes in the country. A 2009 article from *Legatus Magazine* details the religious vocations that grew out of the parish over a period of ten years: twenty priests, twenty-four seminarians, almost two dozen women in vows in religious orders, and ten women in formation in various orders.[16]

When I was in high school, my dad took a trip to Ann Arbor and attended Christ the King for Sunday Mass. I will never forget him coming home and describing the experience. He was blown away. He related how the depth of prayer, the devotion, the working of the Holy Spirit were tangible. Later, when my wife and I lived in Ann Arbor, I had a chance to attend Christ the King myself a few times. It did not disappoint! You can sense the culture of Christ the King as soon as you walk in. There is just something different there than in any other parish I have ever been to.

Often, when we cannot gain traction in trying to renew our parish, it is because we are bumping up against a cultural obstacle that we may not have known was there. Implicitly, operating the way we have for generations has defined the culture of our parishes in ways that can be unhealthy. We have formed Catholics in what it means to be the Church, and often this formation has missed the mark.

Many of our parishes have operated for a long time mainly as places for baptized Catholics to gather together (most) Sundays for Mass and to receive the sacraments. Whether we like it or not, this maintenance mindset in a parish creates a definite culture.

How can you begin to determine the current culture of your parish? Simply ask the following questions — ask them of yourself and of your parishioners:

- What does it mean to be a Catholic?
- What does it mean to be a member of this parish?
- Why does our parish exist?

Culture reflects our answers to these big questions, and everyone has an answer, whether they think they do or not. How do your parishioners answer these questions? That is your parish culture.

For years, the culture of our parishes has largely been focused inward, driven by the maintenance-mode model. Following the Second Vatican Council, with its radical call to go outward and re-Christify the world, too many parishes simply focused inward, enacting changes to the liturgy and governance, looking to parish membership and offertory as benchmarks of success. This emphasis is responsible for some of the decline we are seeing today. The maintenance model seemed to be all that was required of parishes when the secular culture largely supported religious practice. Yet this apparent vitality lulled us into a false sense of security. We mistook high levels of activity in our parishes for overall healthy cultures and never considered looking deeper to see if our parishes were really fulfilling their mission: to form disciples.

In our present cultural reality, the only possible "maintenance mode" for parishes is mission. The secular culture in our world no longer supports religious practice. It is, in many ways, openly hostile to Christianity in general, but especially to Catholicism. What many parishes and dioceses are awakening to is the fact that, in our current secularizing moment, the only way forward is to sell out for mission. For parishes, this will require a complete cultural overhaul — an overhaul that is focused on turning our parishes into what they are supposed to be: missional hubs of the New Evangelization. How do we do that?

Here is the punchline, where it all comes together: In order to renew the Church, we have to renew the parish. In order to renew the parish, *we have to form disciples who can make disciples.* It is that simple. It is never easy, but it is also not complicated. This is our vision with L'Alto Catholic Institute. Parishes are renewed and transformed when the people who comprise them experience deep and lasting conversion through becoming missionary disciples.

> *In order to renew the parish, we have to form disciples who can make disciples.*

You might think of changing parish culture like making good barbecue. As I understand it, barbecue developed because it was an easy way to make cheap meats taste delicious. Using low heat and slow cook times, you can tenderize even very tough meats. The key is time. You've got to let it cook for hours. Cultural change is like that, because it involves the transformation of attitudes and hearts. It is not the work of a moment.

This kind of transformation is difficult, and, because of that, too often left untried. Aiming at the total overhaul of the parish culture has to be the end goal, or else many parish leaders, who deeply desire the renewal of their parishes, will never begin because of the difficulties they encounter. To effect such a change will take not a week, or even a year or two, but will be the work of the next ten years. This is the inherent difficulty in parish renewal. We are facing a problem that should have been fixed twenty years ago. There is an urgency to the task in front of us. Yet, the antidote will also take time. There is no way around this problem, and any attempts at "shortcuts" will only lead to false starts.

We need to begin with this big-picture vision of a complete cultural overhaul, from focusing inward on maintenance to moving outward toward mission and forming disciples. Only a goal that big will inspire the work that will be required.

It might only be slightly hyperbolic to say there is really no such thing as "parish renewal" per se. There is only the transformation of people who then live out that transformation in community and mission. Any true renewal of a parish culture must make as its first goal the renewal of parishioners themselves as intentional disciples.

WHERE ARE THE DISCIPLES?

As I have talked to leaders in the pro-life movement over the years, I have heard a shift in emphasis in much of their language. While there is still plenty of focus on legislative action,

I am hearing many leaders in the pro-life movement reflect on the need to change hearts in addition to laws. Without the renewal of hearts, without people understanding the value of every human life including unborn life, any changes that are made to legislation will just be overturned by the next generation. The battle may be won with strategies, but the war is won with conversions.

This brings us to the fundamental problem that is plaguing our parishes right now: Too few Catholics are intentional disciples of Jesus Christ. It's not the music, the preaching, the liturgy, the greeters, the Religious Education program, or the parish picnic. None of those things is the core issue, and so none of these things can be the core solution. The problem is that for too long, parishes have not explicitly invited people to hand over their entire life to Jesus Christ, helped them grow into the fullness of Christian maturity, and then sent them on mission to go do the same for and with others. Before we can turn our attention outside our parish walls to reevangelize the secular world, we have to first deal with this crisis of a lack of intentional discipleship in our pews.

Before we can turn our attention outside our parish walls to re-evangelize the secular world, we have to first deal with this crisis of a lack of intentional discipleship in our pews.

If we fix this problem, we can fix our parish cultures.

Pope Saint John Paul II put it this way: "It is more necessary than ever for all the faithful to move from a faith of habit, sustained perhaps by social context alone, to a faith which is conscious and personally lived."[17]

If a culture is the sum of the attitudes of actual people, it is only when a significant percentage of a parish is intentional, missionary disciples that it will really begin to approach cultural renewal. If that is not our sole goal in everything we do, we will just be shuffling around our strategies and getting nowhere.

A parish that wants to renew itself must have a singular focus on forming disciples. It must be abundantly clear to staff, laity, clergy, *everyone*, that the entire life of the parish, it's raison d'être, is to form disciples of Jesus Christ, and there must also be an equally clear understanding of how that happens in the parish. It is only then that the renewal we seek can move from a surface-level reality to become the actual living culture of the parish.

This is actually great news, because it gives us a concrete place to begin our renewal efforts. Lasting change, real change, comes from this more personal focus on helping individuals walk into a life-changing relationship with Jesus Christ. In other words, if you want large scale, macro culture change in your parish, you have to start by getting micro.

What was so markedly different about the culture of Christ the King parish that made it as formative and impactful as it is? It is not just that they did Catholic things or that they had a plan for evangelization or that there was good music. The long-time pastor, Father Ed Fride, was very clear on what happened. He said, "The spirituality of the parish, in which a personal relationship with Jesus is continually stressed, is key ... a living, active relationship with Jesus Christ is encouraged."[18]

When a culture is forged by dynamic, joyful, creative disciples living their entire lives for the Lord, there is a compounding factor. When a parish has hundreds, even thousands, of on-fire missionary disciples totally sold out on living a radical call to holiness and bearing fruit with their lives, amazing things can happen. If your parish was like that, how would it change the way it looked to outsiders, felt to insiders, and operated for leaders? Can you even imagine your parish operating like that? Is it difficult to even conceive of?

Does the thought even make you a little nervous?

Every parish is called to be this kind of community. Look at the incredibly fruitful culture of the early Church as described in the Acts of the Apostles. The first Christians were a joyful community of disciples bringing thousands to the Lord. The Church today still has the same vocation. This is the lofty calling every parish shares.

Becoming a missional parish, focused on seeking and saving the lost, is the "destination" for every parish in our current cultural climate. Focusing on forming disciples is the path to get there.

BEYOND BUZZWORDS

Before we go any further, let's define some terms. So far, we have been throwing around a lot of big Churchy terms without defining how we are using them in this context. Let's get on the same page about what this book means when it is using them.

Intentional disciple. Missionary disciple. Evangelization. New Evangelization. Renewal. Encounter.

I'll say it: All of these words have become mere buzzwords in the last few years. Too often ministries and parishes seeking growth and renewal seem content to add a few of these to the mission statement without taking any concrete steps to real, transformative renewal.

The corporate world is notorious for creating a host of such buzzwords. They clutter conversations by using complex terms to describe simple ideas. Buzzwords tend to obfuscate dialogue and make outsiders feel like what is being discussed must be far beyond their understanding. Such words create a clear culture of who's in and who's out, even if the matter described by a buzzword is pretty straightforward.

Many of us Church insiders tend to let buzzwords get in the way of communicating clearly and simply.

Many of us Church insiders tend to let buzzwords get in the way of communicating clearly and simply. Words are important. That fact was drilled into me as a philosophy major in college. Half of my studies, it seemed, were focused on defining terms. Words delineate, they explicate, they untangle. They help us take an idea in our head and present that concept to someone else. They can also obscure if we are all using the same word but are not clear about what exactly we mean by it. If we as a Church are going to continue to use words like "disciple" and "evangelization," then we need to define what exactly we mean by them. Sadly, buzzwords become so overused that they often lose their original verve. This is a problem, because these words actually do convey a message that the Church today needs to hear.

Change in our parishes cannot come about simply because we have a new thesaurus. We cannot keep doing the same old things and just put new words on them. So, in order to avoid that, let's get some clarity around what we mean by these two key words: evangelization and discipleship.

Evangelization

Now, when we hear the word "evangelization," a lot of preconceived notions might come to our head. Knocking on doors, street preaching, giving talks — all are examples of evangelistic activity, but they themselves are not evangelization *per se*. For our purposes, in this book, I want to focus on two meanings the Church ascribes when she uses the term "evangelization."

First, the Church often uses the word "evangelization" to refer to a specific moment in the process of conversion. This is the moment when an invitation is issued to an individual to live a life of intentional discipleship.

Second, the Church also uses the word "evangelization" to refer to the entire process whereby she accomplishes her God-given mission to make disciples. This is the meaning I want to consider in more depth.

Why does the Church exist? Poll Catholics today, and you will get as many answers as individuals. To spread justice, to celebrate the liturgy, to care for the sick, to gather the community, etc. Yet what is the Church's identity, at her core? What does she exist for? Pope Saint Paul VI answers this question boldly in *Evangelii Nuntiandi*: "Evangelizing is in fact the grace and vocation proper to the Church, her deepest identity. She exists in order to evangelize."[19]

What Paul VI is saying there is not just, "The Church should evangelize," or, "We should focus more on evangelization right now." He says that evangelization is the Church's "deepest identity," because evangelization springs from the Church's very essence as the Bride of Christ. She exists in order to bring souls to her Spouse. This means that if the Church stops evangelizing, she fails to live up to her ultimate purpose. It could even be said that it is not so much that the Church *has* a mission but that the Church *is* a mission.

How does she fulfill this mission to evangelize? According to Paul VI, "The Church evangelizes when She seeks to convert."[20] The Church is evangelizing whenever she is intentionally calling believers and nonbelievers to greater holiness through repentance, a process of conversion which is lifelong. She proclaims the message of who God is, his very inner divine life, which is the true meaning and fulfillment of the human heart.

To evangelize is to meet someone where they are and invite them into the Divine Adventure — into the ultimate relationship that satisfies every longing of the human heart. It is to take this incredible invitation and lovingly place it in the current context of someone's life, whether they are a mystic or a sinner.

The key here is to artfully combine both the invitation to conversion while meeting someone where they are. As Aristotle said, virtue is found in the golden mean.[21] Without compassionate awareness of where someone is, the message of repentance becomes shrill and preachy, unable to actually transform hearts. At the same time, if we never invite people to turn away from their sin and give their hearts to Christ, we run the risk of not fulfilling our call to spread the Gospel.

One of the reasons modernity does not understand the loving nature of the Church's call to repentance is because we have done a very poor job of telling our story. The invitation to change, to conversion, is always issued from the Father's heart, through the Church's maternal

The invitation to change, to conversion, is always issued from the Father's heart, through the Church's maternal love for each person.

love for each person. With Pope Saint John Paul II, the Church cries out to each and every soul:

> It is Jesus that you seek when you dream of happiness; He is waiting for you when nothing else you find satisfies you; He is the beauty to which you are so attracted; it is He who provoked you with that thirst for fullness that will not let you settle for compromise; it is He who urges you to shed the masks of a false life; it is He who reads in your heart your most genuine choices, the choices that others try to stifle.
>
> It is Jesus who stirs in you the desire to do something great with your lives, the will to follow an ideal, the refusal to allow yourselves to be ground down by mediocrity, the courage to commit yourselves humbly and patiently to improving yourselves and society, making the world more human and more fraternal.[22]

The truth that the Church proclaims is that transformation in Jesus Christ is an invitation to the fullness of life. Only a few hundred years after Jesus walked the earth, Saint Athanasius proclaimed, "God became man so that man might become God."[23] At Baptism, each of us is initiated into a family relationship. Baptism begins a process of transformation that will restore us to become again like God. As Jesus said to the woman at the well, "The water that I shall give will become in him a spring of water welling up to eternal life" (Jn 4:14). The Church has long held this doctrine: Salvation is about us becoming like God. Yet too often, this stunning reality is overlooked in our preaching and teaching.

To evangelize, then, is to welcome people into a relationship with God that will transform them utterly, from the inside out. The adventure of a human life is wrapped up in the question of whether we will move from the absence of God into the fullness of God. The process of evangelization means meeting someone exactly where they are in that adventure and inviting them into the next step.

As C. S. Lewis wrote in his famous sermon, *The Weight of Glory:* "There are no *ordinary* people. You have never talked to a mere mortal. Nations, cultures, arts, civilization — these are mortal, and their life is to ours as the life of a gnat. But it is immortals whom we joke with, work with, marry, snub, and exploit — immortal horrors or everlasting splendours."

When we are evangelizing, we are choosing to take the future glory of someone else and make it our own mission. We do this not just because the Church needs more members or donations are down, we do it because it is their ultimate destiny and because their Father craves that relationship with them. We do it, in other words, out of love of God and love of neighbor.

You may think that making this distinction is an unnecessary aside, but, really, it is crucial for us in this moment, with so many parishes talking about renewal, to be very clear about what building evangelizing parishes actually looks like. These distinctions drive behavior, the kind of initiatives and strategies we choose to implement or not implement.

This distinction is also important because it has to do with motivation. The question "Why evangelize at all?" is one that has to be answered by us as parish leaders. Working in a parish, giving your life to ministry has to be about loving others. We have to look deeply into our own hearts and ask ourselves seriously why we do what we do. Are we willing to shoulder the weight of our neighbor's glory?

When we do not see the big picture — the full story of salvation history — our processes of evangelization can become shallow. That's when we begin to settle for less, and our goals become relegated to making people "engaged members of our parish" rather than the image and likeness of God. Yet our job is to proclaim "what love the Father has given us, that we should be called children of God; and so we are. ... Beloved, we are God's children now; it does not yet appear what we shall be, but we know that when he appears we shall be like him" (1 Jn 3:1–2). This is our identity as the Church.

Discipleship

Before he ascended into heaven, Jesus entrusted the mission he had received from the Father to his followers. He told them, "Go therefore and make disciples of all the nations, baptizing them in the name of the Father and of the Son and of Holy Spirit" (Mt 28:19). That was his job, and he was handing it on to his followers.

When the waters of Baptism come crashing down on the forehead of every new Catholic, this story of salvation history becomes their story. We are welcomed back into right relationship with God and the divine life comes rushing into our soul. The likeness to God, which was lost to Adam and Eve when they sinned, is restored, and we are forever marked as disciples of Christ, called to bring others to discipleship.

In the last handful of years, the word "disciple" has become increasingly popular in the Church. It speaks to a needed emphasis that has been missing for too long. But what makes a Catholic a disciple or not a disciple?

Consider two different encounters Jesus had with individuals during his public ministry: the encounter with the rich young man, and the call of Simon Peter and his brother Andrew.

In the first encounter, a rich young man comes to Jesus, asking what he must do to gain eternal life. It turns out that this rich young man is, in fact, incredibly moral and righteous. Jesus invites him deeper, saying, "If you wish to be perfect, go, sell all that you have and follow me." Instead of answering the call, the young man "went away sorrowful" (Mt 19:16–22). Now, we do not know exactly what happened to the rich young man later. Certainly, he has much life left to live, and we can hope that he changed his initial decision. There is, in fact, one tradition in the Church that the rich young man is the Gospel-writer Mark. But the point here is that this young man was not a disciple.

In the second encounter, Jesus sees two brothers, Simon and Andrew, fishing. Jesus tells them he wants to make them fishers of men. The Gospel says, "Immediately they left their nets and followed him" (Mt 4:20). Simon and Andrew were willing to take the risk of being disciples of Jesus. Being a disciple is not just about activity, though it generally involves that. Yet activity is accidental to the nature of discipleship. What is at the core is the decision to follow Jesus completely.

A disciple is someone who does what Simon and Andrew did when they left their nets and followed Jesus. A disciple is someone who has made, in Saint John Paul II's words, a "personal and conscious decision" to give their entire life to God. To ask whether someone is a disciple or not is not to judge their holiness. The term "disciple" is not a synonym for "saint." Rather, asking if someone is a disciple is asking whether they have had an encounter with Jesus Christ that has led to the decision to follow him with their whole life.

> A disciple is someone who has made, in Pope Saint John Paul II's words, a "personal and conscious decision" to give their entire life to God.

This distinction is especially important in the current context in our parishes, where we have entirely baptized congregations, yet relatively few intentional disciples of Jesus Christ. If we want to carry on the mission of Jesus, we need to do as he did. And Jesus spent his entire public ministry encountering individuals and inviting them to discipleship.

To the woman caught in adultery, "Neither do I condemn you; go, and do not sin again" (Jn 8:11).

"Zacchaeus, make haste and come down; for I must stay at your house today" (Lk 19:5).

To the rich young man, "Sell what you possess ... and come, follow me" (Mt 19:21).

Baptism is a critical first step, and for many Catholics, that happened in infancy. In the early Church, for most Christians, the decision to follow Jesus as a disciple was followed by Baptism. Today, this order is reversed. Now, we need to make sure we do not skip over the all-important step of helping Catholics actually become disciples. As Pope Benedict XVI put it in his very first encyclical, "Being Christian is not the result of an ethical choice or a lofty idea but the fruit of an encounter with ... a person."[24]

The lack of discipleship that is more common is the core issue. Many of the other issues you might be experiencing as a parish and in our Church at large sprout from this one deep problem: not enough Catholics are intentional disciples. When you see surveys that find that almost 30 percent of Catholics say that they believe in a higher power, but not really the God of the Bible,[25] you know there is a cultural ill present in the way we are forming people. Have we allowed God to remain an impersonal, distant authority somewhere off in the universe?

The decision to be a disciple is always made in the context of a relationship.

The decision to be a disciple is always made in the context of a relationship. As Jesus says, "Believe ... in me" (Jn 14:1). To become a disciple is to respond affirmatively to the invitation to have a personal relationship with God. This is where evangelization and discipleship are closely tied to one another. One of the reasons we have so con-sistently failed to make disciples as a Church is because we have not led frequently enough in our evangelization efforts with the relationship with Christ.

Jesus Christ, risen from the dead, is more alive today than you or I, and he wants us to live our lives in a transformative relationship with him. Each doctrine, each moral teaching of the Church, flows from and back to this invitation.

Now, it should be stated that this relationship is more than just a feeling. It means the complete transformation of our lives into Jesus' image and likeness. As the *Catechism of the Catholic Church* puts it: "By faith, man completely submits his intellect and his will to God. With his whole being man gives his assent to God the revealer. Sacred Scripture calls this hu-man response to God, the author of revelation, 'the obedience of faith'" (CCC 143). This complete personal entrustment of one's self can only be done as a gift of self to another person, in the context of relationship, not just to an abstract theory or moral decision. It is at the very heart of our faith. From Pope Benedict XVI again: "Faith thus takes shape as an encounter with a person to whom we entrust our whole life."[26]

In case you are still a bit concerned that this is not a Cath-olic idea or somehow not in line with our tradition, I will leave you with this quote from Thomas à Kempis, author of the Catholic classic, *The Imitation of Christ*:

> You cannot live well without a friend, and if Jesus be
> not your friend above all else, you will be very sad and
> desolate. Thus, you are acting foolishly if you trust
> or rejoice in any other. Choose the opposition of the
> whole world rather than offend Jesus. Of all those
> who are dear to you, let Him be your special love. Let
> all things be loved for the sake of Jesus, but Jesus for
> His own sake. Jesus Christ must be loved alone with
> a special love for He alone, of all friends, is good and

faithful. For Him and in Him you must love friends
and foes alike, and pray to Him that all may know and
love Him.

A Conscious Decision

Whether the disciple perceives a moment where such a personal and conscious decision to make Jesus the center of his
or her life has been made, becoming a disciple is always the
culmination of a process of grace working on the soul over
time.

I had a friend in college who grew up in a very Catholic
family. Not only were her parents practicing Catholics, but
they were real disciples of Jesus Christ, having participated in
a charismatic covenant community for many years. For her,
however, it was a point of insecurity that she had never really
had a *big conversion moment*. As she had listened to famous
speakers over the years recount their testimonies of straying
far from morality and Christ, only to return in a moment of
brilliant clarity, she wondered if she was somehow missing
something essential to the Christian life, this moment of complete conversion.

Now, knowing her as a friend, I could tell very clearly that
she was a disciple. Her life was completely driven by growing
in love of God and neighbor, living the Catholic life to the full.
Her relationship with God was very personal, very close, and
was bearing fruit in many different ways. For her, though, an
unease remained. Had she made, in Saint John Paul II's words,
a decision to follow Jesus which is "conscious and personally
lived"?[27]

The answer is yes. Hers may not have been as intensely
focused on a particular moment as mine was, kneeling in a
church after a morning confession when I was eighteen years
old, but she had made a decision at some point.

My wife has a similar story. She cannot point to a single
moment in her life in which she made the one, big, conscious

decision to follow Jesus. Rather, she can look to seasons in her life where grace was pulling her deeper to greater holiness and mission. She was like the older brother in the story of the prodigal son. She never left home, but there was greater need of a deepened relationship, and through the invitations of the Father, she was brought deeper and deeper into a more personal walk with Jesus.

Recently, my family drove across the country as we moved to our new home just south of Denver. One of the highlights was the moment we crossed the Colorado border. A big "Welcome to Colorful Colorado" sign greeted us on the interstate as we crossed over from Nebraska. It was a joyful and definite moment.

In contrast, a couple of years ago, we took a trip to Chattanooga, Tennessee, to do some hiking. The drive there was gorgeous, winding through the Appalachian mountains. Chattanooga, though, is really close to the Tennessee-Georgia state line. We noticed, as we drove along, that our GPS showed us hopping into Georgia and then back into Tennessee every so often. We were never really clear on when we crossed the line. It was only when we stopped to assess our location by looking at a map that we realized we had crossed into a new state.

This is kind of how it is with discipleship. Sometimes, disciples can point to the one singular moment when they became a disciple of Jesus Christ. Sometimes, it is more difficult to say exactly when it happened. Always, though, the disciple should be able, if a personal, conscious decision has taken place, to see the overall arc of how God took over their life. They can point to a season or a multitude of decisions that led to the orientation of their life toward trying to grow in relationship with Jesus.

Too often, we place an outsized importance on that first conversion moment in our faith journey. Really, the crucial thing is the movement to place Jesus at the center of our life. It involves the handing over of our entire self. Saint John Paul

II put it this way: "Conversion means accepting, by a personal decision, the saving sovereignty of Christ and becoming His disciple."[28]

Whether the decision to follow Christ happens in a moment or through a particular season of life, if we pause and reflect, we can point to a journey of grace that led us to the fundamental disposition of our heart being to live for Christ. Even for Saint Paul, the gold standard of a radical conversion story, the decision to leave his old way of life and follow Jesus was a process that took time. If I look at my own conversion story, even though the choice to change my life happened in a moment, the actual change was the working of years.

The crucial marker of a disciple is that they can look at their heart and say, not, "Am I perfect?" but, "Has God arrested my heart and life completely?"

Can we say with Saint Paul, "It is no longer I who live, but Christ who lives in me" (Gal 2:20)?

Having laid the foundation in terms of the real crisis at hand in our parishes and the antidotes this book will propose, namely, creating a culture of intentional, missionary discipleship in our parishes, we can finally address the core question of this book: How?

Over the next five chapters, we will walk you through the four keys, which we laid out in chapter 1. These are the simple strategies L'Alto Institute uses when we work with parishes. They are designed to help any parish begin the process of cultural change, and these principles are applicable in any parish context.

CHAPTER 4

The First Key: Cast Vision

In the process of cultural renewal, we first have to ask ourselves: Where do we begin?

In 1997, Apple was at a crossroads. Earlier that year, its famous visionary founder, Steve Jobs, had returned to the company after being forced out years earlier. He came back to an organization that was struggling. Apple had been the leader in personal computing and innovation, but after a string of failures, it was hemorrhaging, with many experts believing the company to be past its prime and potentially even dying. Jobs quickly decided that Apple's brand, long one of the strongest and most recognizable in the world, needed to be strengthened in people's minds through an ad campaign. This campaign would become one of the most renowned in history.

In a speech unveiling the new campaign, Steve Jobs revealed that the heart of strengthening the Apple brand was a celebration and rededication to Apple's core value. In a stirring address worth looking up on YouTube, Jobs told Apple employees:

> Our customers want to know who is Apple and what is it that we stand for. Where do we fit in this world? And, what we're about isn't making boxes for people to get their jobs done, although we do that well. We

do that better than almost anybody in some cases. But Apple is about something more than that. Apple, at the core, its core value, is that we believe that people with passion can change the world for the better.[29]

"Think Different" was the tagline of this new ad campaign, which celebrated innovators throughout history. Positive and hopeful, the first TV ad began with the now legendary phrase, "Here's to the crazy ones." The campaign positioned Apple as the company where people who believed in a better tomorrow brought their purchasing power and led to a revitalization of a slowly dying company.

A decade later, Apple had rebounded almost completely through innovative products like the iPod. Then, in 2007, Jobs announced the launch of the iPhone, a product so unique that it has changed culture and the world irrevocably by its very existence. Today, Apple sits again as one of the leaders in technology.

There is no doubt that the Catholic Church's "brand" today is seriously wounded. Decades of scandals and lackluster experiences in parishes have left the Church that Jesus Christ founded wounded and reeling, hemorrhaging her members, and, often, not perceived as a credible witness to the Gospel. Frankly, in many people's minds, the Catholic Church is not a place to encounter the love of God and love of neighbor. They see the Church as an aging institution with outdated laws and rituals. Even our dedicated parishioners often view their parish just as a place to receive the sacraments and attend events, not as mission outposts of the New Evangelization.

Jobs' example is powerful and instructive for our purposes because his vision, communicated through the "Think Different" ad campaign, was a reminder to everyone, both Apple employees and consumers, of the core of who Apple really was. His vision for the future of Apple was grounded deeply in the core of what had made it a technology leader in the past.

If we are going to change the culture of our parishes, the very first step must be getting people to reconnect with the Catholic Church's core value, her *Why*. We have the greatest reason for being in the world; we alone have been entrusted with helping people encounter the one relationship that can satisfy their hearts. Yet, too often, that *Why* is not the driving force behind what we do as a parish.

This is why we need to begin, as Steve Jobs did, with casting vision. The first battle we have to fight in cultural renewal will be for how those in our pews conceive of and understand the purpose of our parish.

Parishes are called to be places where people's lives are radically changed in encountering Jesus, and where they are supported in intentional community as they grow in holiness and spread the Gospel. If we want that to be our parish, then we need to craft a clear picture in people's minds of that identity and how we plan to get back to it.

The first battle we have to fight in cultural renewal will be for how those in our pews conceive of and understand the purpose of our parish.

To lead culture change is about being able to see something no one else sees, a new vision, and then to externalize that vision in such a way that people can see it with you. It is not about dragging people where you want them to go but inviting them to gaze at the horizon with you, and come to desire it just as you do.

As we have mentioned before, tweaks are not going to cut it. True cultural change within the parish demands that we allow the Holy Spirit to breathe a new culture into our parishes. This is not going to be accomplished by one or two people acting alone; it must be a collective movement of committed parishioners moving in this new direction together. The call to move our parishes from maintenance to mission has to permeate every aspect of parish life, and this can only be done by first casting vision for where we are going and why.

This chapter is going to walk through what we consider to be the three steps of leading with *casting vision*. They are:

1) Have a clear vision that is based on God's own vision for your parish.
2) Communicate that clear vision to your whole parish.
3) Let your vision lead the way in decision-making.

STEP 1: Have a Clear Vision

Simon Sinek, one of the most well-known thought leaders for organizational health in our time, and a bestselling author and speaker, has said, "All leaders must have two things: they must have a vision of the world that does not exist and they must have the ability to communicate it."[30] Eye has not seen what God has ready for the parish that commits to large scale renewal, but we have to be decisive and have a clear vision for the journey that needs to take place.

Here is the good news. You do not have to invent the vision for your parish. Having a clear vision is not about you or me deciding what we would like a parish to be. Our vision for our parish must be rooted in the mission that Jesus Christ himself puts before his Bride. This means first of all remembering that the parish is missionary at its core. It shares the same call as the universal Church, to go and make disciples of all nations.

We are still in the early days of this new missionary age, so having a vision for where we are going requires that each parish be a bit — well — visionary.

Ultimately, the work of renewal is about God's grace, and we cannot engineer the perfect parish on our efforts utilizing our earthly wisdom. We do have to think, though, as we are trying to bring our parishes to mission, about what that looks like. Sadly, though I can think of a few, we do not yet have a lot of great examples of truly missional Catholic parishes. We are still in the early days of this new missionary age, so having a vision for where we are going requires that each parish be a bit — well — visionary.

Times of great change always require this kind of visionary thinking, the ability to see possibilities that are categorically different from what has worked in the past. Henry Ford is famously reported to have said, "If I had asked people what they wanted, they would have said faster horses."[31] Few people at that time could have dreamed of the Model T.

For our Church today, taking on this kind of visionary thinking is actually about recommitting to the vision Jesus Christ himself put before the Church and incarnating it in our present context. The mission statement and goal for our parish has already been provided for us by our Founder. For us, radical culture change is actually about rediscovering our identity in light of the words of Christ: "All authority in heaven and on earth has been given to me. Go therefore and make disciples of all nations, baptizing them in the name of the Father and of the Son and of the Holy Spirit, teaching them to observe all that I have commanded you; and behold, I am with you always, to the close of the age" (Mt 28:18–20).

As parish leaders, if we have not first allowed the Lord to shape our hearts according to this clear vision, then we will not be able to communicate it. The people we serve crave authenticity, and they will be inspired by seeing us burn to have that vision accomplished. People want to follow great leaders who know where they are going and are willing to sacrifice to get there. They are inspired by it.

To be that kind of leader, we have to first let the Holy Spirit shape our hearts.

Pentecost

I have always been fascinated by Saint Peter. Apart from Jesus, he is one of the most vivid figures in the Gospel. Out of all of the Apostles, we seem to have the clearest sense of Saint Peter's personality. His actions through the Passion and Resurrection are particularly fascinating. Denial at the fire outside Jesus' trial. Awe and amazement at entering the tomb and finding the Lord's body gone. Reconciliation on the shores of Galilee.

Peter's story is one of earnest failure, which is why I think I cherish his witness so much. His good intentions, but also his weakness, come through extremely clearly in the Gospel accounts. In light of his humanity and stumbles, I get goose-bumps whenever I read the first papal homily, in Acts 2, after the Holy Spirit comes down upon the early Church at Pentecost. Peter goes from being frozen in his own fear and inadequacy, to becoming a bold prophet of the Gospel, rivaling the brazen brilliance of even the Old Testament prophets. To the assembled devout Jews gathered for the Feast in Jerusalem, he thunders, "Let all the house of Israel therefore know assuredly that God has made him both Lord and Christ, this Jesus whom you crucified" (Acts 2:36).

The people's reaction? "Now when they heard this they were *cut to the heart*, and said to Peter and the rest of the apostles, 'Brethren, what shall we do?'" (Acts 2:37, emphasis added).

Their hearts are rent open, allowing them to see a new vision for reality. The Holy Spirit cries out in their hearts in that moment that *Jesus Christ is Lord*. Peter's words alone cannot do that. Only the power of the Holy Spirit, which he received moments earlier, can.

Faith, the power to believe in the revelation of God, is a gift from God himself. The grace of conversion is just that, a grace. If we are to cast vision in our parishes, this is not just about announcing a new corporate strategy. We are not just trying to inspire people to action, we are trying to inspire them to change, and that takes grace. It takes the power of the Holy Spirit.

If you are trying to bring about a new reality in your parish or in your ministry, you cannot do that on your power alone. Everything you do needs to be covered in intercessory prayer, and you need to be consistently begging for more of the Holy Spirit in your life. I strongly encourage you to ask your parishioners to pray every day for at least a full year for the Spirit to come down in power and lead you to renewal. See what happens. I guarantee the Lord will increase not only the faith of your parishioners, but your own faith as well.

> *Everything you do needs to be covered in intercessory prayer, and you need to be consistently begging for more of the Holy Spirit in your life.*

On the day of Pentecost, three thousand people were baptized. That is the kind of impact the Holy Spirit can work through us when we are open to it.

STEP 2: Share the Clear Vision

I have a secret: Change requires … change. And people fear change.

If you have ever tried to implement changes in your parish, you know all too well the resistance it can bring. This is called "inertia." In physics, this is the property of matter by which it continues in its existing state of rest or uniform motion in a straight line, unless that state is changed by an external force. In parish life, inertia is the property of some long-time parishioners that makes them complain whenever you do something that is not "the way we have always done things here."

How do you overcome cultural inertia in parishes? How do you take God's vision for your parish and help others interiorize the same vision? The secret is that, before you start making changes, you have to spend time communicating the clarity you have to the rest of the parish. You have to share the vision. This requires time, intentionality, strategy, and a lot of prayer.

Start with Why

Simon Sinek's book *Start with Why: How Great Leaders In-*

spire *Everyone to Take Action* describes how people buy into something when you tell them why they should. This is because "why" is much more powerful than "what." As persons, we are driven by *Why* more than anything else.

In a nutshell, you could summarize Sinek's book with his phrase, "People don't buy what you do, they buy why you do it."[32]

Sinek uses the example of Apple as an organization that starts with why. Apple has been so successful because all of their communications always emphasize why they do what they do. They want to shake things up, to "Think different." Everyone gets that about Apple. Only after making sure you are really clear on their core value do they then move to their *How,* their strategy. They make change and shake things up by creating user-friendly, simple, and beautifully designed tech products.

When it comes to the mission of the Church, our call to form disciples, we need to make sure everyone knows this is our raison d'être. It needs to be central in everything we do. Those in the pews need to know how everything we do relates back to that why. There needs to be a clear hierarchy of communication in sharing this vision that keeps this vocation central.

Sharing the vision means infecting others with this vision for the parish. That requires communication. In fact, it takes over-communication. We need *Sharing the vision means* to bring people along with us in *infecting others with this* our desire for culture change, in- *vision for the parish. That* stead of seeing those who don't *requires communication.* yet share the vision as obstacles. It is unfair to imagine that every person in the parish is going to adopt a new vision overnight just because we retooled the mission statement.

One of the keys to clearly communicating a renewed vision for your parish is to avoid the temptation to jump to the practicals too quickly. The *how* and the *what* of parish renewal are crucial, yes, but we have to begin with talking clearly about *why* our parishes are desperately in need of revitalization around a commitment to evangelization.

About a year ago, I was traveling with my family and needed a coffee shop to work in for the day. I discovered a local community center that not only had a place to work but also an indoor playground for kids. How ideal, I thought! The kids could blow off steam and I could get work done. Win-win.

We arrived at the community center and found it to be a massive, repurposed warehouse that had auditoriums and an indoor soccer field in addition to the playground and coffee shop. We were greeted by a friendly person at the door who welcomed us and showed us the ropes, telling us if we had any questions to just holler. We felt incredibly welcomed by everyone we met.

It was only after about an hour there, while walking to the bathroom, that I put the pieces together. The community center was actually an outreach of a local church. On getting back to my table, I asked the greeter sitting nearby where the actual church was.

"Oh," she said, "this is our church building. We gather in the auditorium every Sunday."

I was fascinated. The massive construction must have been an eight-figure building project, yet, all of the facilities were clearly oriented toward the outside community, rather than toward the church members themselves. I could not help but wonder how they had raised the funds. Most church capital campaigns are about creating spaces that the membership exclusively will enjoy. How could you convince people to give millions of dollars to build something that was not primarily for them?

For me and my young family, bumping into this community center was such an overwhelmingly positive experience of welcome that when I arrived home, I called the pastor. I needed to know how he had crafted this kind of culture in his church, both in terms of convincing everyone to build outward-facing facilities but then also inculcating within everyone a latent instinct for welcoming and community.

Even though the church was not Catholic, clearly the leader of this community was one who knew how to create a dynamic culture of evangelization.

The pastor revealed to me that, for years, their church gathered every week in a hotel ballroom, slowly growing from about twenty members to over a thousand. They had always believed that their community had a particular charism for evangelization and loving the local community, but they were located in the most secular part of an already secular college city. He and his senior leadership team had conceived of the community center as a way to bring value to the lives of young families in their neighborhood who needed a gathering space in the frigid winter months in particular. They found the warehouse and hired an architect to scope out the project. As I had guessed, he revealed that the architect told them it would be a significant project, more than the young church could afford by far.

"How did you raise the money, then?" I asked.

You could almost hear the pastor's smile. "For an entire year, I preached every single Sunday about how our core value as a community was that we exist not for ourselves but for our neighbors. That whole year, we had people praying like crazy for this project. After the end of the year, we started asking for money and had the entire amount raised in six months." Here is a lesson for every parish seeking to radically transform its culture. This is how we share a clear vision for this transformation.

As parishes, if people get really committed to our why, that we exist in order to evangelize, then they will dedicate their entire lives to making that happen. Every missionally fruitful parish knows why it exists and makes decisions about what it does and does not do based on that why.

I am convinced that, even as we make our proximate goal to change the culture of our parishes by forming those in our pews as disciples, it has to always be clear that the ultimate purpose and vision for the parish is more than that. Ultimately, even intentional discipleship is a pit stop on the journey to the final destination of reconciling all things to the Father in Jesus Christ. A good analogy is marriage. In marriage, the intimacy of the couple is always paramount; if that does not exist, nothing else can. However, marriage is ultimately about more than just the couple; it is about bearing fruit, to generate new life in others, both spiritually and physically. The work done to strengthen the inside is not only for its own sake but ultimately for the sake of others.

Churches become mere social clubs when the missional vision is not constantly reinforced. Even churches with good discipleship formation run this risk. The missionary nature of the Church has to be the *Why* behind everything we do as parishes. Too often, though, there is not a clearly articulated *Why* behind much of what we do. How much time do we spend communicating *What* we are doing without clearly explaining why or even how? Parish bulletins, announcements, etc., are almost always focused on the *What:*

"We have an event coming up for this feast day."

"Come to the parish picnic."

"Sign up for a holy hour."

"Join this Bible study."

If we set people on fire for the sweeping vision of a parish transformed, it will be easier to get buy-in for the specific efforts it will take in order to get there.

If we are going to create a culture of missionary discipleship at our parish, we need especially our core leaders convicted not just about what we are doing but why we are doing it. It is hard to get people motivated about coming to the next event or volunteering if that is all we ever talk about, but if we set people on fire for the sweeping vision of a parish transformed, it will be easier to get buy-in for the specific efforts it will take in order to get there.

A culture that lacks a strong and compelling *Why* begins to drift toward using the language of obligation to motivate people. When people are not internally driven to work toward the common cause, those of us who work in parishes tend to default to "should" language. We expect people to behave a certain way just because we are there and we think they should.

- *Why should I come to Mass on Sunday?* Because you are supposed to!
- *Why should I volunteer for that ministry?* Because the ministry needs volunteers!

We can build new initiatives, try different things, attempt to innovate, but we are not going to change people's lives unless we start with why.

- Come to this night of adoration because we want you to encounter Jesus. Your heart is made for him and will be restless until it knows him.
- Join a discipleship group because Jesus has an amazing plan for your life and wants you to grow into the fullness of who God made you to be.
- Lead a ministry at our parish because your relationship with Christ is not just for you but is meant to bear fruit. As Jesus said, "I chose you and appointed you that you should go and bear fruit" (Jn 15:16).

In setting a vision for your parish, there should be a clearly defined *Why, How,* and *What* that everyone understands. Here is a made-up example of how a parish could effectively communicate using the *Why, How, What* model:

- *Why (identity):* Jesus Christ came that we might

have life, and we want everyone in our parish boundaries to know that life to the full.

- *How (strategy):* We form disciples who have given their entire life to Jesus by helping them encounter Christ, grow in Christ, and be sent by Christ.
- *What (tactics):* We offer Alpha so people can encounter Jesus personally, small groups to help people grow as disciples, and missional formation to prepare them to be sent.

In our current cultural context, parishes must be prepared to row upstream. If you have ever been in a canoe or a rowboat, you know that it takes everyone working together, rowing in unison. As parish leaders, when we start to make decisions and communicate decisions this way, we start to get everyone rowing in the same direction, instead of a thousand different oars trying to get to their own small alcove in the river.

Too many parishes have convoluted mission statements that are simply descriptive. These mission statements express not where the parish wants to go, but where they are right now. An example might be, "We are a welcoming community gathering in worship and service to grow in … " In this era of needed revitalization, parishes must have simple and clear mission statements that point to the future, about who they know they are called to become. Parish leaders must be willing to articulate to the entire community: *Here is where we are being called by God to go.*

As we talked about before, *Evangelii Nuntiandi* puts before us God's vision for his Church: "The Church exists in order to evangelize." Does everyone in your parish know this? If that is the mission of the Church, then it is also the mission of your church. If we interviewed twenty parishioners, would they be able to articulate that purpose clearly?

Just think about the tires of your car: If they aren't properly aligned, it can cause damage over time. Parishes work the same way. Even small misalignments in vision mean that parishioners will categorize their parish community into various identities. Some might envision the parish as just a social club, others see it as a place to receive the sacraments, and still others look to the parish as a social justice outreach center. These are all things a parish should do, of course, but leading renewal is about getting everyone motivated around the one mission of the Church: to make disciples and then set the world on fire through evangelization. We need to start with helping everyone see that reality.

With whom are we trying to share our vision first?
As parish leaders, we become used to having complaints arise when we try anything new. So, over time, we start to anticipate criticism whenever we do anything, and we become less confident. I hear this all the time when I work with parishes: "Oh, we tried something like that and we caught so much flak. We'll never make that mistake again!" Or, "We can't do that. The (group of long-time parishioners) will get all over us for that!"

When we are communicating our vision, sensitivity to naysayers is normal. But we can't let the naysayers dictate our decisions, or we will never reach the goal of total cultural renewal within the parish. The key is to try to talk to the people who can be galvanized to lead change with you. When we seek to bring about renewal, we are innovating (even though we are hearkening back to age-old principles), and in order to innovate, you have to talk to the people who are ready to innovate with you.

In sharing our vision about culture change in our parishes, we want to talk in language that the innovators and early adopters will be passionate about. They can then lead the charge for the rest of the parish. The temptation is to try to keep everyone happy, including those who are entrenched in their own way of doing things. This is an ineffective method, and usually a waste of time and energy. Instead, I encourage you to let the people who are ready to go run with you. Try to block out the negativity of the naysayers, while remaining pastorally sensitive to individual lives.

If you are unsure of where to begin as you seek to share your vision with the whole parish, turn to Appendix 2 for some practical examples.

STEP 3: Let the Vision Lead the Way

Jesus Christ, forever with his Church, wants to give us the power of the Holy Spirit to make disciples. That is our whole mission as a Church. Why do we so rarely do it, then?

"Mission-drift" is a phrase used to describe the movement of an organization, consciously or not, away from its core mission. It is, at its core, a crisis of identity. When organizations forget who they are, what they were originally created to be, they begin to chase every seemingly good idea that comes along, eventually drifting far away from their original calling. Every organization, if it is not guided by a clear and compelling vision of who it is at its very core, will begin to experience mission-drift.

Sadly, many (perhaps most) parishes in the United States today have experienced profound mission-drift. Almost every parish I have ever encountered is extremely busy, doing a lot of very good and important work. But when you consider that the mission Jesus Christ gave to his Church was to "make *disciples* of all nations," then you start to see how many good things have piled up that are not at the core of our mission.

Mission-drift is actually another form of sloth, like we mentioned before, or *acedia*. Josef Pieper, in his book *Leisure: the Basis of Culture*, defines the deadly sin of acedia as a sort of sadness at the good that is marked by a resistance to doing what we were meant to do — a spiritual laziness that does not have the will to be what God desires.[33] More often than not, acedia is not marked by inactivity, but by a sort of hyperactivity that does everything except the one thing necessary, because the one thing necessary is hard. If we want to cast the vision for our parish, we have to combat this tendency to *acedia* wherever it rears its head.

Making disciples is hard. Creating lasting culture change is hard. It is a lot easier to just keep doing what we are currently doing, to continue to build a maintenance culture, than to try to align everything we are doing as a parish with the calling of Jesus Christ to form disciples.

Yet our parish is not ours. It is God's. He established a Church for a reason, because he wants to fill everyone in the world with the divine life. Having a vision, then, is not about pridefully deciding what we want our parish to be. It is about humbly conforming our desires to God's, who wants us to make disciples.

Don't Jump to Tactics Too Soon

How do we create the discipline in our decision-making to begin to receive God's vision for our parish? It is not enough simply to have a sense of who we are. We need strategy and tactics in order to start aligning ourselves to God's vision and fulfilling our mission. If vision is the destination, then strategy is the route,

The strategy is the *How:* the larger, overarching goals that will get us to the vision.

The tactics are the *What:* the practical steps that will accomplish the strategy.

Once we have cast a vision for why we exist as a parish, then we can move into strategy. Strategy is not yet tactics, it is not yet what we are doing to make those strategies happen. Strategy involves laying plans, setting big overarching goals that we then use tactics to try to achieve. When planning for renewal, we should always reverse engineer from vision to strategy to tactics. Often when parishes start to fail, it is because an inordinate amount of their attention is focused on tactics alone, and not enough on vision and strategy.

As Catholics, we do not need to worry much about crafting our strategy. Just like vision, strategy has been provided for us. It is called the "catechumenal model" or the process of evangelization. We will talk more about this strategy in the next chapter.

For us as parish leaders, discernment is needed to determine the *What* or the tactics. How can our parish best form people according to each step in the evangelization process? This requires prayer and serious thought in the specific cultural context of your parish. What worked somewhere else might or might not necessarily bear fruit in your context.

Every decision that we make as a parish should be in reference to our core mission. Have the discipline to be willing to say no to things that do not serve that primary end in some fashion. Have the courage to try new things that could advance that mission in new and dynamic ways. Then, when you talk about your mission, when you try to cast this vision of a parish fully committed to forming disciples, work backwards from vision to strategy to tactics.

Having laid out the vision, we can now get to the second key in creating cultural change in a parish around a vision for forming disciples: crafting and rallying around a clear path to discipleship.

CHAPTER 5

The Second Key: Craft a Clear Path to Discipleship

Not that long ago, I was contacted by a large, vibrant, suburban parish that wanted help building a culture of discipleship. Wanting to do a little research before our meeting, I glanced through the parish's website to gather some preliminary information. A website won't tell you everything about a parish community and what it is like, but it can reveal a lot. Blazoned on the homepage was the parish's mission statement: "We exist to form intentional disciples of Jesus Christ."

I was encouraged. Clearly, someone had read a book on parish renewal, and the parish leadership were committing to a new path by codifying their goal in a simple and accessible mission statement. I even wondered if they really needed my help. Maybe they already had this whole renewal business figured out! As I kept browsing the website, though, I could tell that they were not quite there yet. In fact, the website concerned me a bit because, though the mission was laid out very clearly, it was not at all clear how it was actually being carried out.

About a week later, I met with the parish leadership in person. We had a great time talking parish renewal and discipleship. They expressed their sincere desire for their parish to become more missionally effective. They especially wanted their parish to reach out to young families and young adults, who were drastically underrepresented in their congregation.

Toward the end of the conversation, I unpacked my big question: "What is your parish mission?"

"Easy!" they answered. "To form intentional disciples of Jesus Christ."

"Great," I said. "I love the simple clarity of that mission. Now, how do you do that?"

"Well ... " Everyone shifted in their seats uncomfortably, staring down into their lattes.

The president of the pastoral council stepped in. "Well, we do tons of stuff! We have a men's ministry, we have a great St. Vincent de Paul outreach, we do Bible studies ... " He listed several more programs the parish had.

I decided to take them a little deeper. "Let's say I am a 35-year-old father of two who just moved back to the suburbs from the city. I am busy but spiritually curious. I stopped going to church in college, but I want my kids to grow up in the same faith that I did. How does your parish help me become a disciple?"

They just stared at me. The blank looks on their faces said it all. The parish was doing a ton, and had even articulated a desire to form disciples, but no one really knew *how* that was going to happen.

Because the mission of a parish is to form disciples, it should be abundantly clear to each leader and each parishioner how the parish actually accomplishes that mission.

If you take only one lesson from this book, focus on this second key: crafting a clear path to discipleship in your parish. Because the mission of a parish is to form disciples, it should be abundantly clear to each leader and each parishioner how the parish actually accomplishes that mission.

HOW DO PARISHES FORM DISCIPLES?

Often when Catholics talk about forming disciples, it can sound like a great mystery. We act like it is some big riddle, as if the Church has never attempted to form disciples before or thought about how that happens. As Ecclesiastes reminds us, though, "There is nothing new under the sun" (Eccl 1:9). The Church has been trying to form disciples for centuries, even if we often lose focus on that as our core mission. Because of this, we don't have to look too far to discover pretty clearly how parishes can form disciples.

Forming disciples is a process. It is the sum total of the journey to become the fullness of who God made us to be. The Church summarizes this process of evangelization in what is called the "catechumenal model" or the model used for the formation of adults wishing to enter the Church through the Rite of Christian Initiation for Adults (RCIA). This model spells out exactly how leaders in the Church should operate if they want to help people become missionary disciples.

This articulation of the evangelization process is so crucial that the *General Directory for Catechesis*, the guiding document for all evangelization done in the Church, says: "Given that the *missio ad gentes* is the paradigm of all the Church's missionary activity, the baptismal catechumenate, which is joined to it, is the model of its catechizing activity."[34] All of the Church's catechizing or evangelizing activity should be modeled on the catechumenate.

I like to simplify it in these four steps:

1) Pre-Evangelization
2) Evangelization
3) Discipleship
4) Apostolate

In these four steps, the Church looks at people in different stages of their faith journey and asks, "If the mission of the

Church is to evangelize, what should we do for someone based on their stage of spiritual progress?" The answer is always one of the four steps above.

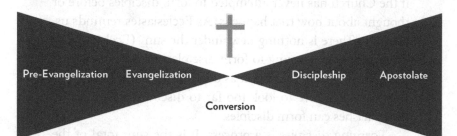

Pre-Evangelization   Evangelization   Discipleship   Apostolate

Conversion

Note on the chart above the moment when conversion happens. Everything before that moment of conversion is narrowing in on that conscious decision. Everything after leads to expanding the full Christian maturity and confidence of the individual so that they can become a great saint and bear fruit in the lives of others. This is the model for all evangelization. Yet in almost every parish I have ever visited, the first two steps, pre-evangelization and evangelization, are treated as an afterthought. This is a problem, because these are the steps which actually lead to that moment of conversion.

THOSE WHO DON'T PLAN, PLAN TO FAIL

We need to bring *intentionality* to our work of forming disciples in parishes.

It is not that parishes *never* evangelize or that they *never* welcome people or that they *never* disciple people. Most parishes try to do some of these things at least some of the time. The problem is that we do not walk intentionally with individuals on a journey through the whole process. Within most parishes, our individual efforts are siloed from another, and parishes have so many of them that it becomes unclear what purpose each initiative serves.

For many parishes, especially larger ones, the number of

ministries at the parish becomes a point of pride. You'll see it in the annual end-of-the-year stewardship report: "We have 157 ministries as a parish!" Yet think about this from a parishioner's point of view, especially a parishioner who is new — or maybe just returning — to the practice of the Faith. Can you imagine trying to pick which ministry to get involved in? Often it is better for a parish to have five really impactful and fruitful ministries than a hundred ministries that are burning out volunteers and failing to help participants go deep.

Especially in larger parishes, it can be tempting to launch a renewal effort by multiplying ministries and activities in the hope that something will work out. Some pastors are not that great at delegating and never allow their parishioners to try new things to reach people. Others just say yes to every new idea that comes along, hoping to throw enough stuff against the wall that something eventually sticks.

Yet it is precisely busyness that can sometimes obscure the fact that a parish is not bearing fruit by forming disciples. Because there is a lot of activity, a parish can be convinced that it is really thriving, when it may in fact be slowly dying. Remember, the mission of any parish is to form disciples. Discipleship is not defined by involvement in parish life, "engagement," or volunteering. It is characterized by a relationship. Rather than seeking to create yet another program, it's important to look for this benchmark within your parish. Is there a committed and growing relationship of love present between individual parishioners and God? That is the mark of discipleship.

Discipleship is not defined by involvement in parish life, "engagement," or volunteering. It is characterized by a relationship.

In discerning how our parish is being called to form disciples, we need to drill down into a few key areas of strength and focus our energies there. The movie *Remember the Titans* presents a good example of this. It tells the inspiring story of a recently integrated high school in the turbulent 1960s. Their football team overcomes the obstacles of racial tensions to build real friendships and, eventually, win the state championship. At the beginning of the movie, the new head coach of the football team, played by Denzel Washington, is questioned by his assistant coaches about his thin offensive playbook. He tells them, "I run six plays, split veer. It's like Novocain. Just give it time, it always works."[35]

Anyone who follows football knows that a lot goes into running six plays well. It means eleven different players working together, each doing their job perfectly, to carve up yardage. It also means everyone is working hard. But instead of working hard without a strategy, they have prioritized a handful of things that they know work really well to help them achieve their end goal.

We need more churches with that kind of laser focus, willing to commit to a simple, clear strategy for forming disciples. This clear path to discipleship should include a few things, done really well, that will intentionally walk people through the entire process of growth into mature discipleship. Conversion is perpetual; we are never done growing. Additionally, not everyone who becomes a disciple in your parish will do so just by following the pathway in a clear, precise order. As parishes, though, we really need a more purposeful and, overall, *simplified* approach to our strategy for the full process of evangelization.

Charting this clear path to discipleship allows us, the entire community, to cast one big net together, instead of a thousand single fishing lines sporadically.

A discipleship pathway also builds clarity around our approach to ministry for leaders to understand and opt into. Charting this clear path to discipleship allows us, the entire community, to cast one big net together, instead of a thousand single fishing lines sporadically. Which do you think will ultimately be more effective in making us "fishers of men"?

A CLEAR PATH THAT WORKS

To display what a clear path to discipleship looks like in a parish context, I reached out to one of the parishes that I think really "gets" this part of parish culture change: St. Patrick's in Maple Ridge, British Columbia, near Vancouver. Their Director of Discipleship Formation, Julia Hanley, has spent much thought and effort helping to move her parish toward operating in this clear path paradigm. As a result, this parish has one of the most comprehensive, effective, and simple clear paths to discipleship I have ever seen. When I asked her why she started utilizing a clear path in her parish, she said,

> We realized that, while our mission statement (to form missionary disciples) was focused, our behaviour was not. ... We desired a pathway prioritizing the individual's relationship with Jesus. If this was the focus, then we would have to facilitate the accompaniment of every person on their faith journey. We wanted everyone to be bought in to our newly focused approach to the mission, and [we] knew that a shared experience and common language would foster a parish culture with momentum and apostolic zeal that extends beyond the church walls.

Here is what the clear path to discipleship looks like at St. Patrick's.

ST. PATRICK'S PARISH

Principles of the Discipleship Formation Pathway

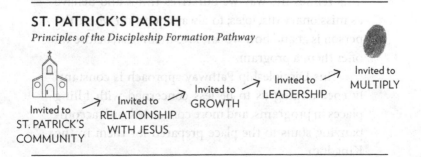

Invited to
ST. PATRICK'S
COMMUNITY

Invited to
RELATIONSHIP
WITH JESUS

Invited to
GROWTH

Invited to
LEADERSHIP

Invited to
MULTIPLY

This is an effective description of a discipleship pathway, because it uses welcoming language that focuses more on principles than on programs. It literally "invites" people into the journey of discipleship. At the same time, it makes it clear that each initiative or program serves this larger journey of conversion and does not replace the fact that the real work is happening interiorly in individuals.

St. Patrick's wisely uses the clear path as a tool and not an end in itself. Julia shared with me:

> In its application, each principle has an associated "method" (typically a program/series, etc.) that must meet a list of conditions. The conditions are concerned with the content of the method — i.e., whether it is kerygmatic, clear and simple, welcoming, etc. These conditions, which must all be met in order for a program to "pass" at the parish are agreed upon in light of the way we evangelize people (based on where they are at). The conditions are in place to guarantee that the methods are formative, with the set expectation that the method increasingly challenges the disciple in holiness and mission the farther along in the pathway that the person progresses.
>
> Because of our focus on the principles of conversion that one person experiences, we can select methods which effectively meet the needs of the collective. This refines the way we ourselves think and behave as missionary disciples; to always question where the person is at and how we can love them best, before we offer them a program.
>
> This Discipleship Pathway approach is constantly encouraging us to be less concerned with filling places in programs, and more concerned with accompanying souls to the place prepared for them in the Kingdom.

Julia is a young apostle, only in her twenties, yet to talk to her is to be inspired by what God can do through Spirit-led leaders. She is sharp, strategic, and understands the big picture behind parish evangelization in a way few do — even many who are twice her age.

CLARITY IS ABOUT SAYING "NO"

Let me lay out for you an all-too-common scenario. A pastor goes to a big conference or reads a book on parish renewal. He is convinced by the call to renewal and knows something different needs to happen at his parish. He begins the effort in his parish by forming an evangelization and discipleship committee. What happens next? That committee introduces a new program.

The new initiative starts off with great energy and purpose. After some time, though, it loses steam, and the pastor loses interest. He is so bogged down by the million other things going on in the parish that he cannot devote enough attention to really make his new committee or program successful. The committee continues to meet every month but never does anything, and the volunteers eventually give up and quit. The program continues to run indefinitely but never really makes the impact it could. Though his conscience gnaws at him a bit, the pastor contents himself with thinking he has at least checked the evangelization box. Evangelization remains one silo in a parish full of silos and never brings about the culture change which inspired the pastor in the first place.

I will never forget an experience I had when working full-time as a director of evangelization and catechesis at a parish of 6,000 families. We had a launch weekend for a popular program that helps people encounter Jesus personally. This was a centerpiece of our renewal initiative, an important outreach that we wanted to be a "pump" for everything else that followed. I did all the right things: I scheduled a pulpit announcement that I gave personally, set up a table in the narthex, had laptops for sign-ups available along with paper forms. We had volunteers handing out invitation cards to everyone walking past the table so they would at least have something to spark their memory and remind them to sign up. It was a full court press.

I got to the narthex to set up our table early. In the spot I had planned to set up our table, the best high traffic area, there were already two other tables set up with information for other initiatives that weren't even related to our parish specifically. I turned around to see my plan B spot filled by a fundraising effort. That weekend, another group had received permission (without my knowledge) to pass out books to people coming out of Mass. Our table was relegated to a corner. There were so many things going on that weekend that, after my pulpit announcement, there were five minutes more of additional announcements.

Everything going on that weekend at our Masses was good. Nothing was sinful or heterodox. But it was distracting our parish from focusing on our one, core mission: to form disciples. Sure, I was annoyed that it was my personal initiative that was being crowded out, but more importantly, I saw how the busyness of our parish was creating so much noise that evangelization and discipleship simply could not be prioritized. If one thousand things are all equally important, then, really, nothing is important.

Building a clear path to discipleship begins by saying "no." If you are trying to proceed with a renewal effort and are not shutting down a few ministries or saying no to a few people who want to use narthex space, then you will dilute your efforts. Nothing changes if nothing changes.

Building a clear path to discipleship begins by saying "no."

Saying no is tough; it takes courage. People might be mad at you. They might not understand why their ministry or program is not being prioritized by the parish. Wherever possible, gentleness in leadership is a gift. This means the ability to hear someone and try to explain, to talk about the *Why* in such a way that they might be able to see the bigger picture. At the end of the day, though, not everyone will get it. But think of the souls that might be lost because we do not have the courage to set off boldly and chart a new course!

If you have too many programs going on in your parish that are not about your clear path to discipleship, you will have a difficult time getting people to commit to the programs that do serve that clear path. People only have so much time; if they are going to get involved with something, they want it to matter. Yet if they are faced with a smorgasbord of fifty choices, many people will end up just choosing "None of the Above."

FOR EVERYTHING, A PURPOSE

Hyperactivity is the enemy of fruitfulness because it prevents us from measuring initiatives to determine whether they are actually achieving their objective. How do you apply metrics to 157 ministries across a parish? You simply can't. To bear fruit, we need to prioritize a few key things; pour a lot of resources, attention, and training into them; and then continually improve them based on what is actually fulfilling the mission.

It is important to note that the strategic goal of every ministry is not to form disciples. No one ministry or program can do that. Rather, each ministry should fulfill a strategic objective within the clear discipleship pathway for the whole parish.

Every initiative we invest in as a parish should have a particular audience in mind based on their spiritual journey. And each initiative should be designed to accompany them, to build relationships, and, as Pope Saint Paul VI urges, "to convert." In other words, each initiative should be part of an overarching parish strategy to help people move to the next stage in their relationship with God.

These stages might include the following:

- To build trust with those who are not religious.
- To provide an occasion for someone to encounter Jesus personally.
- To mature those who have had a conversion moment into full disciples of Christ.
- To send disciples on mission.

In many of our parishes, the reason we have begun to drift away from our core mission to form disciples is because we are being tempted to focus on good things that are not the best thing. Saint Ignatius of Loyola provides two sets of principles for discernment. In the first set, he lays out principles for beginners, describing how the devil will try to tempt them away from following the Lord, either by keeping them comfortable in sin, or by making the good seem so difficult that they are tempted to give up altogether.

For "devout souls," though, he describes how the devil has to get somewhat craftier. Because he knows he cannot tempt the devout soul by mortal sin, he comes to them as an "angel of light," tempting them by something good that is not the very best thing. Since he cannot directly tempt them not to pray, maybe he can do so by keeping them so busy that they feel they have no time to pray.[36]

We need to keep this firmly in mind in our parish renewal efforts. There are so many good things to be done that we wear ourselves out chasing everything we *could* do, yet we fail to prioritize the one mission that Jesus Christ gave us: to make disciples.

PEOPLE, PROCESS, PROGRAMS

People do not like to be turned into projects or to feel used. I remember when I was growing up, the bane of my dad's existence was the telemarketers who always seemed to call right around dinner time. They had that gift for dialing *just* as the family was about to say grace. It drove him nuts.

We hate telemarketers because they bother us, but we also hate them because they are so clearly just using us. We are simply a number to them. They have done the analysis and they know if they make a certain amount of calls per hour, the math turns in their favor and they will make money. On an even deeper level, we hate being contacted by college friends we have not spoken to in ten years, who want us to join their multi-level marketing network. We feel like our personal connection and trust in someone is being manipulated.

When we utilize a clear path to discipleship, it can be tempting to start turning people into projects. When evangelization becomes about numbers or pushing people in our parishes around like they are pawns on a chessboard, we know we have fallen into the tempta-tion to make people serve our own work, rather than seeking to be at their service.

When evangelization becomes about numbers or pushing people in our parishes around like they are pawns on a chessboard, we know we have fallen into the temptation to make people serve our own work, rather than seeking to be at their service.

The reality is that people are messy. We need to balance the fact that we need to be intentional about our strategy with the fact that people's lives do not follow an ordered little path to discipleship. It is one of the reasons that we need everything we do to be imbued with the proclamation of the Gospel; otherwise, we are likely to fall into the trap of thinking one program or event will change everybody's lives and we can check the box off for that step.

A phrase that helps me keep in mind the need to put people first is "People, Process, Programs." Keeping these three properly prioritized is crucial for utilizing a clear path to discipleship effectively. Every program that we implement should be at the service of our process, or our clear path to discipleship, and our process itself should be at the service of our people. It is no good to have a clear path to discipleship if we are just treating it like the Disciple Maker 2000. Hand-offs between different programs in the process need to be done in such a way that they are human and relational, not robotic and impersonal.

The key to making the entire process work is accompaniment. Some of that comes from leaders understanding the clear path deeply enough to bridge people through the various steps, but some of it comes through having individuals in our parish who can personally walk with people in friendship as they move through the process of becoming missionary disciples.

"People, Process, Programs" can also help us to avoid a programmatic mentality in our ministry of just trying to throw programs at things to fix problems. In the movie *My Big Fat Greek Wedding,* the Greek dad of the main character hilariously puts Windex on every injury, thinking it is a cure-all. His famous line is, "Put some Windex on it." In parishes, our line could be, "Put a program on it." Often, it seems we think that as long as we have a running program for each age group, we have done our jobs. When it comes to culture change and evangelization, we cannot be content with simply putting a program on it. We have to really evaluate everything we are doing for fruit, not just output. It is not about how many people we put through a program; it is about how many people are becoming disciples.

The key is to keep the actual process at your parish as simple and clear as possible. Do not try to do everything at the same time. Prioritize a few very effective initiatives. In a clear path to discipleship, the outcome we are looking for is not so much what we do, but what God does in people.

In walking with parishes to begin to implement culture change, through my organization L'Alto Catholic Institute, I have found the phrase "Win, Build, Send" to be a much more accessible way to articulate the catechumenal model. This concept of "Win, Build, Send" has been popularized in Catholic circles by the campus ministry group Fellowship of Catholic University Students (FOCUS), but it has existed for a long time in Protestant circles. It perfectly lines up with the steps of the catechumenal model:

Win → Pre-Evangelization and Evangelization
Build → Discipleship
Send → Apostolate

Usually, when we craft language to communicate these steps to the parish, we try to use more "audience-facing" language. So the clear path as articulated to the parishioners would be, not "Win, Build, Send," but something like, "Encounter, Grow, Go."

In the next chapter, however, we will take a look at each of those steps with some deeper considerations on how a parish can accompany individuals through the journey of conversion. It is possible here that you are inspired to start crafting a clear path to discipleship right now. I recommend that you wait to read the next chapter. There we will talk about some of the principles behind the Win, Build, and Send steps and will provide practical guidelines for building a clear path in your parish.

CHAPTER 6

Win, Build, Send

In this chapter, we are going to do a practical deep dive into the process of "Win, Build, Send" in the context of a Catholic parish. This is designed to give you a sense of how to help people navigate each phase of the clear path to discipleship. It is important to go into some detail about the mindset surrounding each of these steps in the formation process so that we can make the correct tactical decisions in accomplishing each step.

PART I: Win

Jesus turned and saw them following him and said to them, "What do you seek?" And they said to him, "Rabbi" (which means Teacher), "where are you staying?" He said to them, "Come and see."

— John 1:38–39

Pre-evangelization

The idea behind pre-evangelization is pretty simple. Each human heart is made for the Lord. However, often there are obstacles in people's hearts to being able to really receive the message that God loves them and wants to fill their hearts if they turn to him and make him the center of their life. Pre-evangelization refers to all of the preparation, especially the removing of obstacles, to make way for receptivity to the Gospel message. It is a crucial part of the "Win" step in a clear path to discipleship.

Pre-evangelization refers to all of the preparation, especially the removing of obstacles, to make way for receptivity to the Gospel message.

I grew up attending public schools, and by eighth grade, I was beginning to get in enough trouble that my parents hoped that sending me to a Catholic high school would help to straighten me out. (Spoiler alert: it did not.) Even though I begged them not to, they enrolled me for my freshman year at the local Catholic high school.

Not only did the Catholic high school not "straighten me out," in fact, I would have hated to reveal to my parents how lackluster the formation at my school really was, especially in my theology classes, in which we learned hardly any theology at all. Years later, following my conversion, I majored in theology and philosophy in college. I absolutely inhaled the Church's teaching. Teresa of Avila, Thomas Aquinas, Augustine, Anselm, Catherine of Siena, all of them were a breath of fresh air to me. Their brilliance, combined with their deep faith, opened my eyes to the rich intellectual heritage of our faith. I was being changed just by what I was studying. It was exciting and invigorating.

I decided in one of my theology classes that I wanted to be a high school theology teacher. Frustrated that my own experience of intellectual formation as a teenager had been so lacking, I wanted to open students' minds to this amazing landscape of Catholic theology that I had missed. After a couple detours following college, I finally got a job teaching at an amazing Catholic high school in southeast Michigan. My first assignment: to teach moral theology to 150 sophomores.

To be honest, the first year was a tough one. In addition to learning the rigors of lesson-planning and classroom management, I struggled to make the kind of impact in the lives of my students that I so desperately desired to make. Even my (I thought) well-researched, formulated, and articulated arguments for the Church's positions on various moral topics seemed to be falling flat. Those students for whom I had the greatest heart, the disenchanted ones, the ones most like I had been in high school, either did not care what the Church taught or were openly hostile to her teachings.

At the end of one extremely frustrating week, I stopped on my way home to get my hair cut. The wait was thirty minutes during the post-work rush, and I settled into my seat in the waiting area, closed my eyes, and started to pour out my troubles to God.

"Why can't I reach them?" I implored.

No answer.

I just waited there in silence, searching heaven for some wisdom, when a passage from the Gospel popped into my mind. I quickly Googled the Parable of the Sower and the Seed and drank in the biblical wisdom. In this parable (found in Matthew 13), Jesus lays out a scenario where a sower is scattering seed on different types of soil: a path, rocky ground, thorns, and good soil. Only the seed scattered on the good soil takes root and bears fruit. On the path, the birds steal it right away; on the rocky ground, it shoots up quickly but does not last; the seed scattered among the thorns grows for a time but eventually is choked out by the thorns. The apostles later ask Jesus to explain the parable. Jesus says:

> When any one hears the word of the kingdom and does not understand it, the Evil One comes and snatches away what is sown in his heart; this is what was sown along the path. As for what was sown on rocky ground, this is he who hears the word and immediately receives it with joy; yet he has no root in himself, but endures for a while, and when tribulation or persecution arises on account of the word, imme-

diately he falls away. As for what was sown among
thorns, this is he who hears the word, but the cares
of the world and the delight in riches choke the word,
and it proves unfruitful. As for what was sown on
good soil, this is he who hears the word and understands it; he indeed bears fruit, and yields, in one case
a hundredfold, in another sixty, and in another thirty
(Mt 13:19–23).

I realized that the Truth was not taking root in the hearts of
the young people I was trying to reach because, simply put, *it
couldn't*. There was a lot of soil that needed to be tilled first.
I prayed all weekend about what to do. I realized one of the
core problems was that I was trying to teach objective moral
tenets to teens who did not really believe in an absolute objective morality.

I returned to the classroom on Monday armed with three
weeks of lesson plans designed to teach my students that objective morality was not only real and necessary, but that our
hearts actually long to know the path that will lead to true
flourishing. The first week, we read Aristotle and Aquinas and
talked about the human longing for an ultimate fulfillment
that we call happiness. In week two, we tackled moral relativism, showing it to be self-refuting and an incomplete, disor-
dered way of viewing human action. Finally, we talked about
the concept of freedom and, utilizing John Paul II, showed
that the law is ultimately ordered toward our freedom. Using
only philosophy, we spent three weeks tilling the intellectual
soil, trying to dispel the relativistic notions that the teens had
imbibed from the surrounding culture.

By the time we got to the big reveal, the punchline, that
Christian morality, revealed by Jesus Christ and expounded
upon by the Church, is really about showing us how to live life
to the full, I found a much more receptive audience. When we
started going back to the moral dictates of the Church, even

on some of the more culturally controversial topics, much of the animosity and disdain had dissipated.

How does this relate to our work in parishes? In order to win people to a relationship with Christ, we cannot begin with catechesis, or even often with evangelization. Evangelization, meaning the proclamation of the Gospel and the invitation to the response of conversion, will fall on deaf ears and hard hearts unless we first spend time tilling the soil.

Evangelization, meaning the proclamation of the Gospel and the invitation to the response of conversion, will fall on deaf ears and hard hearts unless we first spend time tilling the soil.

Pre-evangelization needs to utilize truth, beauty, and goodness in order to prepare people for discipleship. These three attributes of God attract the human heart. They all interrelate and intersect, and each is an indispensable need of the human heart and a motivator for our restless hearts to come to finally possess absolute Truth, Beauty, and Goodness in heaven. The beauty of a mountain vista, the goodness of Mother Teresa, and the truth of Aristotle's ethics all have the power to open the soul to receive Divine Revelation.

Errors in evangelization generally come from the temptation to emphasize only one of the three transcendentals and abandon the other two. Goodness without truth becomes relativism. Beauty without goodness becomes profane. Truth without goodness becomes dry and uninspiring, and so on.

Pre-evangelization is meant to walk with individuals through the various, complex movements of the mind and heart that lead into the choice to become a disciple. The reality is, in our parish context, the pre-evangelization phase accounts for more of the individuals we encounter than we may realize — including both visitors and even our "regulars." This means pre-evangelization is really about the kind of milieu you are creating at the parish. Does the culture you are building arouse curiosity and build trust in people who do not have faith?

Because building this pre-evangelistic culture at your parish is so important, I have outlined "four A's" to help you strategize how to get there:

1) **Appeal to the heart.** Each person possesses a longing for abiding happiness and true fulfillment. The anxious longing in our heart for true meaning is a compass pointing straight to God. Pre-evangelistic efforts can begin with calling out the fundamental human longing for happiness, meaning, and purpose. Encourage individuals to consult their experience to find within themselves the echoes of the eternal. There are many in the post-modern world who, deep down, are wondering, "What is the best way to live? How can I find happiness?" We know people are seeking a lifestyle that will bring peace and joy — just consider the growing numbers of people involved in movements like veganism and CrossFit. Catholic life should be presented in a way that appeals to this part of the human heart.

2) **Appeal to the intellect.** While you and I know that faith and reason go hand-in-hand (a Catholic priest proposed the big-bang theory[37]), for many in our culture, a perceived discrepancy between belief in God and science can be an obstacle to faith. Be prepared with some good answers or good resources to meet people's intellectual doubts. While giving answers is always good, pre-evangelization also requires that we know how to ask the right questions. An example might be, "Why do you think something exists at all when there could just

as easily be nothing?" Appealing to both the heart and intellect can help to arouse curiosity, getting someone to examine their life and open up to the fundamental experience of wonder at reality. This is the beginning of faith.

3) **Address wounds.** It is amazing how often I will listen to someone rant about Church teachings and intellectual questions only to arrive at a core, unresolved suffering that prompted those struggles in the first place. The deep hurts of life can sometimes cause people to lose trust in God. Sometimes, what looks like unbelief is actually pain. Your love and, eventually, when someone is ready, the power of praying together, can help to address the wounds that block the work of the Holy Spirit. Many people have very substantial and real hurts that have caused them to lose trust in the Church or in God. Rebuilding that trust is a prerequisite for spiritual growth.

4) **Always build the relationship first.** Pre-evangelization, before it is anything else, is about relationship. When Jesus meets the woman at the well, he builds a friendship with her, listens to her, and gets to know her, before calling her into a new life. Genuinely love people first, without treating them like a project. Ultimately, this last point is the very best thing your parish can do in order to help people build. If your parish's hospitality efforts could be copied by the local hotel, it might be a sign that your attempts at welcoming people have become too impersonal. People are not going to feel loved and welcomed at your parish just because there was a greeter at the front door; they are

going to feel welcomed, and end up coming back,
if members of your parish make genuine attempts
to build relationships and friendships with them.

A friend of mine is a great pre-evangelist. He is just phenom-
enal at building trust with people. This friend recently told
me about his desire to do more reaching out to other young
families in his parish. One day, during the sign of peace, he
noticed that the couple behind them had a young child about
the same age as his and decided to befriend them. He and his
wife turned around after Mass and invited the couple over for
dinner. The next week, after dinner, over a Manhattan on the
back porch, the husband began opening up about his experience of religion. Even though his family came faithfully to
Mass every week, he revealed that he had no real belief in God.
They just wanted to raise their kids in the Faith. My friend
was able to unpack that unbelief a little more with him and get
him to open up to the possibility that God actually does exist.
If my friend never built that relationship of trust, though, the
husband would never have felt comfortable enough to open up
about what was really going on in his life.

Evangelization

Pre-evangelization is not the end goal, it is only the beginning.
It is not enough to simply arouse curiosity and build trust. At some point, we have to preach the Gospel. Ultimately, our role as parishes is to make disciples of Jesus Christ, and that is done through evangelization.

Evangelization as a moment in the conversion process involves the preaching of the kerygma, or the basic Gospel message, and the invitation to respond by giving your whole life to Jesus.

Evangelization as a moment in the conversion process involves the preaching of the kerygma, or the basic Gospel message, and the invitation to respond by giving your whole life to Jesus. As basic as that sounds, very few parishes in the United States provide opportunities where that can actually happen. Yet this initial proclamation is vital to our work. Essentially, in this call to culture change, to make parishes hubs of the New Evangelization, it is the most important project.

In an ad liminal visit to a group of German bishops, Saint John Paul II put it this way: "The new evangelization begins with the clear and emphatic proclamation of the gospel, which is directed to every person. Therefore, it is necessary to awaken again in believers a full relationship with Christ, mankind's only Savior. Only from a personal relationship with Jesus can an effective evangelization develop."[38]

An easy way to summarize this basic Gospel message is in its four essential movements:

1) God loves you and has a plan for your life.
2) Sin separates us from God.
3) Jesus Christ, in his life, death, and resurrection, saved us from sin.
4) By turning away from sin and toward God and his Church, we can live a new life as adopted sons and daughters of the Father.

To make disciples, we need to infuse everything we do with this proclamation of the Gospel. Here are some practical ways to do that.

Craft Winning Messages
The homily is not the centerpiece of the Mass. The Eucharist is. However, if we want our parishes to be more centered on evangelization, we cannot miss this opportunity to use the homily to preach the Gospel. Too often, we are wasting our unique opportunities to speak to people a message that they need to hear, especially at larger holy day Masses like Christmas, Ash Wednesday, and Easter. Just read the homilies of the

Church Fathers. Almost always, they are centered on the proclamation of the kerygma, and you can tell that these messages were preached out of their lived experience of God.

This call to preach the kerygma extends beyond the homily. Any time a message is delivered in a parish, it should include the proclamation of the Gospel. At the training for new catechists, during the Thank Yous at the parish picnic, in the invitations to join a new ministry, *preach the Gospel.* We need to infuse this initial proclamation in everything we do.

Saint John Paul II had this to say on the subject of preaching and the kerygma in *Redemptoris Missio:*

> In the complex reality of mission, initial proclamation has a central and irreplaceable role, since it introduces man "into the mystery of the love of God, who invites him to enter into a personal relationship with himself in Christ" and opens the way to conversion. Faith is born of preaching, and every ecclesial community draws its origin and life from the personal response of each believer to that preaching. Just as the whole economy of salvation has its center in Christ, so too all missionary activity is directed to the proclamation of his mystery.
>
> The subject of proclamation is Christ who was crucified, died, and is risen: through him is accomplished our full and authentic liberation from evil, sin and death; through him God bestows "new life" that is divine and eternal. This is the "Good News" which changes man and his history, and which all peoples have a right to hear.[39]

If we want to put spiritual fire in the bellies of those we serve, we have to preach the Gospel. Woe to us if we do not!

For a message to be truly kerygmatic, it should end with an opportunity to respond by entrusting one's entire life to

Jesus. John Paul was a master at this. This is why he was able to inspire such hope in people's hearts. He consistently made it a point in his public addresses to speak to the innate human desire for meaning and the freedom that a life lived in Jesus Christ brings. Saint John Paul II probably had plenty that he could have talked about in terms of policies, current events, and cultural issues, but he never addressed a crowd without also preaching Jesus.

Generally, in parishes, we are trying to lead people closer to Jesus through catechesis, or teaching. This is not a bad thing! But as John Paul II wrote in *Catechesi Tradendae*, catechesis finds its role as a complement to the initial proclamation of the Gospel or the *kerygma*:

> Thus through catechesis the Gospel kerygma (the initial ardent proclamation by which a person is one day overwhelmed and brought to the decision to entrust himself to Jesus Christ by faith) is gradually deepened, developed in its implicit consequences, explained in language that includes an appeal to reason, and channeled towards Christian practice in the Church and the world.[40]

A winning message does not always need a microphone. The great proof that God is real and active in our reality is in the impact he makes on the lives of his followers. In most of my evangelistic conversations, I have begun to almost exclusively talk in terms of personal testimony: "Here is what God has done in my life." Stories are a powerful way of communicating the real impact God can have on our lives. We need to normalize a culture of sharing our testimonies in parishes to show people what a life of discipleship looks like.

Prioritize a Main Event

There needs to be one definitive landing place at your parish that everyone knows is the "first step" on-ramp into your parish life. This should not be the Mass. The Mass is ordered toward insiders; it is not meant to be the shallow end of the pool. Yes, it is good to want more beauty in the liturgy, more dynamic and kerygmatic preaching, and greater attempts at hospitality to visitors, but we have to be careful. Making Mass the entry point can lead to gradual shifts in the liturgy in an attempt to be more accessible. This is a misguided approach.

There needs to be one ongoing initiative at the parish that is exclusively about welcoming non-disciples and, in a comfortable environment, sharing with them the basic Gospel message for the first time. This kind of initiative forms the core of your clear path to discipleship. Insiders should know it as the place to invite people, and it should be clear to newcomers and visitors that this is the place where they start.

Programs like Alpha or ChristLife are valuable tools, if used properly and prioritized correctly, that can become a normative part of the discipleship experience at your parish. It is important to note, however, that most people do not come away from one retreat or one program as disciples. It generally takes the kerygma being reinforced over and over again for someone to really respond by giving their whole selves to Christ.

Some parishes recently have found great success by doing a whole parish "immersion" in some kind of evangelization process. This involves basically shutting down everything else to prioritize one evangelization program for a semester or year. This can be a really great way to begin to get everyone going in the same direction. Still, it should not replace the proclamation of the kerygma in everything we do. Few people become a disciple after just one experience of hearing the kerygma and being invited to respond. It takes hearing this basic Gospel message over and over again for most to entrust their life to Jesus by becoming a disciple.

Pray and Get Out of the Way

I was talking with a friend a few years back about how slow the process of evangelization is when you are really walking with someone. We were talking about our mutual experiences of running discipleship groups and how it just takes a long time for people to become disciples.

My friend shared something that has stuck with me ever since. He told me of a Bible study he led for a handful of Catholic guys at varying levels of discipleship. One of the young men in the group seemed dedicated to coming every week, but he stayed at the fringes of the group, not really getting too invested. Week after week, they would all go through the Bible study materials and even have good discussions, but this guy remained a little aloof or detached. Finally, exasperated, my friend pulled him aside after one Bible study and asked what he thought of the group. He said he was enjoying getting to know people and thought the conversations were interesting.

My friend leveled with him. "Do you want to follow Jesus? Do you want to give him your whole life?"

The guy told him yes, but he did not really know what that looked like. My friend led him in a prayer, right there and then, asking for openness to the Holy Spirit and the grace to hand over his whole life to Jesus. It was like they had thrown lighter fluid on a small flame: Whoosh! The guy had such a powerful encounter with God in that time of prayer that his entire life was changed. The weeks of tilling the soil had disposed him to faith, but at some point, the whole process had to be supercharged and supernaturalized by actually encountering the living God.

Not everyone will have an experience like this, but the point is sometimes our own human efforts in evangelizing can only take us so far. Sooner or later, we just have to get out of the way and let the powerful and living God encounter his children personally.

PART II: Build

"So that we may no longer be children, tossed back and forth and carried about with every wind of doctrine, by the cunning of men, by their craftiness in deceitful wiles. Rather, speaking the truth in love, we are to grow up in every way into him who is the head, into Christ."

— Ephesians 4:14–15

You can almost always identify someone who has made the decision to follow Jesus by their hunger to grow. They want to pray better, live better, and serve better, and they usually want to be helped in knowing how. When our parishes are not there to support healthy growth in disciples, one of three things tends to happen:

1) **Growth becomes unhealthy.** New disciples will be working on their own initiatives and may develop their own sense of what spiritual growth looks like, which can often be askew. In order to grow with Christ the vine, they need a trellis, which is what the parish should be.

2) **Growth stalls out.** Alone in their efforts to get closer to the Lord, many would-be disciples eventually either give up out of loneliness and frustration, or they plateau, unable to see new horizons to becoming an even greater saint because they are not being challenged to keep growing.

3) **The disciple finds somewhere else to grow.** I have met multiple people who have told me that, while they came to conversion in the Catholic Church, they eventually left to join other Christian denominations because they found their

Catholic parish to be spiritually uninspiring and painfully lonely as a disciple. Yes, perhaps if they had received a more full formation, they would have discovered that the sacraments are the reason that we stay Catholic. But we should allow ourselves to be challenged by stories like this. Are we doing enough to feed those who have begun to really seek after holiness?

As we consider the crisis of discipleship in our Church, we need to ask ourselves: What if we put the same kind of intentionality and vision into the formation of every baptized Catholic that we do into the formation of priests? Too many of us have slipped into this mentality that the holiness of priests is somehow more important than the holiness of lay people. This is actually an insidious form of clericalism. The call to holiness is universal, and lay people need to be supported in their growth just as priests and religious do.

> *What if we put the same kind of intentionality and vision into the formation of every baptized Catholic that we do into the formation of priests?*

I spent a year in a major seminary in the Midwest, discerning whether I was called to the priesthood. It was a blessed year, during which I was able to study and pray in a more intentional way than life with a normal job often allows for. Ultimately, I was grateful for my spiritual director who helped me to discern that, while I had the desire to give my whole life to Jesus and to evangelize, I had no specific calling to the priesthood.

In the course of my formation studies, a single Church document was referenced more than any other: the Program for Priestly Formation (PPF), a document put out by the U.S. Conference of Catholic Bishops to govern the formation of candidates to the priesthood in seminaries in the United States. The PPF breaks down formation for priests into four major categories: human formation, spiritual formation, intellectual formation, and pastoral formation. It is very thorough in outlining a vision for the kind of man a future priest should be working to become.

Our attempts to help people grow in holiness should include a balance of these same four pillars. That word "balance" is critical, as each of the four pillars is equally important. As parish leaders, we should take this need for formation very seriously. It's a good idea to check in on how we are doing at building disciples, based on the four pillars. Here is a brief examination for parish leadership:

- **Human:** Do we as a parish that helps parishioners grow in the natural virtues? How do we help them develop community and friendship? Do we help them heal? Do we help them find psychological maturity?

- **Intellectual:** Do we make readily available resources that will help expose our parishioners to the rich intellectual heritage of our faith? Do we help them answer common objections to Catholicism from a secular culture?

- **Spiritual:** Do our parishioners know how to pray with their hearts? Do they have daily personal prayer lives? Is that understood as an essential characteristic of discipleship? Are the sacraments, especially confession, readily available so that parishioners can frequent these privileged occasions of grace?

- **Pastoral:** Do our lay people know how to bear fruit? Do we teach them to reach out to their neighbors, family, coworkers, etc.? Are we just telling them to "go," or are we actually coaching them in how to do so most effectively?

In my experience, if parishes are attempting to accomplish this "Build" step, it is largely through intellectual formation. Often, faith formation is relegated to formation of the intellect according to the truths of the Faith. This is important, but it focuses solely on one pillar while ignoring the other three, which leads to lopsided growth at best. We must hold all four pillars in equal esteem and make intentional efforts about each if we truly want to build people into disciples.

Going Together
Groups are key to any "Build" step in a parish. It is not possible for the clergy in a parish to personally direct everyone, but groups, when utilized properly, can help to form people who have newly placed Christ at the center of their lives.

There are a thousand ways to slice the building of a groups ministry in your parish. To go through them all would require an entirely separate book, but any fruitful groups ministry will share some key attributes:

1) It will have well-formed disciple leaders who know how to intentionally pour into others.
2) It will be a place for people to grow in the attributes of a disciple.
3) It will be a place where authentic community can be experienced.

Part of creating a good clear path to discipleship is moving from an events- or media-based Build phase to a groups-based one. This helps intentionally move parishioners through a process of conversion. Often, leaders building a groups ministry become obsessed with which resource they will use. In reality, the resource is less important than the vision you have cast into the groups themselves. Ultimately, it's not important that a group of people went through a Bible study together for six weeks. It's important that a group of people came to rely on one another in their walk toward Jesus. It is not about the gathering, but the growing.

It will be important for you and other leaders in your parish to actually pray through what you want the outcome of your groups ministry to be, because that will drive how you construct them. The temptation is to focus on having groups to fill a need, without clear discernment. Be intentional about how you construct your ministry based on what you want it to do.

One model that has been effective and increasingly common is a combination of mid-size and small groups that serve slightly different purposes. The mid-size groups are primarily about community. They serve to mitigate the daunting nature of big parishes by shrinking things for people and helping them to build numerous connections in the parish. One blog I read talked about how the goal of these groups could be quantified under the idea of increasing the amount of "2:00 a.m. friends" each member has in the church community. To put the idea into my own words, it is this: If your kid gets sick at 2:00 a.m., and you have to run to the hospital, how many friends in the church community could you call to come watch your other kids?[41]

In this model, small groups then become specifically about growth in holiness and discipleship. They are places for accountability, prayer, and study, where serious disciples can gather to build each other up and sharpen one another. This model provides some intentionality to groups ministry. Sometimes, people want groups to do too much. This stratifies the groups a bit more and ensures they will be more purposeful.

Vulnerability is the key to any small group ministry. Without it, your groups will not bear fruit. Our English word "vulnerability" comes from the Latin root *vulnus*, which literally means "wound." To become vulnerable is to expose your woundedness to another. This takes incredible trust and friendship, and it is the indispensable condition of a fruitful Build ministry. Everyone is broken; everyone is wounded. We all have sin and hurt in our life that keeps us from the fullness of who God made us to be. Yet when we keep those wounds to ourselves and never let another into our struggle, we allow the devil to keep us in captivity.

Most people in our contemporary culture need to be taught vulnerability, and they need to see it modeled.

Most people in our contemporary culture need to be taught vulnerability, and they need to see it modeled. After all, our culture teaches us to put on a perfect face for others, especially in Church settings. If you want to build a vision for vulnerability into your groups, which is where real growth starts to happen, you will need to instill it — and model it — intentionally.

Healing and Freedom

My grandpa died of a massive heart attack at age forty-nine, so I never met him. Around forty years after he died, my grandma wrote out her memories of Grandpa George so the grandkids could know more about him. Grandma wrote in her memoirs that my grandpa came from a humble background, but he was an incredibly successful businessman. His core principle for business has always stuck with me as an incredibly important life lesson: "Treat everyone you meet as if they had a broken heart, because in most cases they do."

In this Build step, we cannot overlook the importance of interior healing.

Everyone we meet is broken. The ways we have failed to love and the ways others have failed to love us often result in interior hurts that cause us to act out in self-destructive ways that inhibit our growth. For most people, as they begin to grow more into the image and likeness of God, they also begin to recognize the ways these interior wounds are holding them back. As leaders in parishes, we follow a God who spent most of his time on earth healing people. That means we should be ready to help meet them in this brokenness and help them find interior freedom and peace.

That means that we as parish leaders first have to learn to approach Christ the Healer. Often, learning to encounter Jesus in our own woundedness becomes the greatest source of our strength in ministering to others.

Some brokenness is obvious; you can see the pain that abuse or abandonment has caused people. Others try to hold together an exterior visage of perfection in order to cover up the wounds on the inside. Even some of the most well-formed and prayerful Catholics I know often struggle deeply to really trust God and believe in his goodness because of wounds in their lives. Often, the bitterness and unforgiveness that takes root in our hearts as a result of these wounds keeps us locked in a place where grace cannot penetrate to bring the kind of restoration that Jesus desires.

An essential step in forming disciples is helping individuals to come to full belief in the truth about God and the truth of what he says about them. The *Catechism* teaches that the first stage of sin is the loss of trust in God. Thus, in the Garden of Eden, "Man, tempted by the devil, let his trust in his Creator die in his heart and, abusing his freedom, disobeyed God's command" (CCC 397). Restoration into the full image and likeness of God, then, begins with restoring trust, but this trust is hindered by the interior wounds we all carry.

Our faith teaches us that these areas of brokenness exist "that the works of God might be made manifest" (Jn 9:3). God can heal us, and he wants to, and when we truly let him in to heal us, he sets us free to go and heal others as a result of the healing we have received.

PART III: Send

"You did not choose me; but I chose you and appointed you that you should go and bear fruit and that your fruit should abide."

— John 15:16

There are two earth-shattering conversions that happen in the life of every disciple. The first is the initial conversion we have already discussed, where Jesus is placed at the center of one's life. The second is the conversion to mission, where one gives their life over to not just growing in sanctity, but pouring themselves out into the lives of others.

Many people stop before that second conversion. They are the infinite growers. They have the initial conversion and, out of genuine fervor, spend the rest of their lives learning more about the Faith and seeking to grow in prayer. This is not a bad thing, but it is not the final horizon for those of us baptized into the life, death, and resurrection of Jesus Christ. Instead, each of us is called to multiply our discipleship. Pope Benedict XVI put it this way: "Discipleship and mission are like the two sides of a single coin: when the disciple is in love with Christ, he cannot stop proclaiming to the world that only in him do we find salvation."[42]

However, there are cultural paradigms in many of our parishes that need to be transformed in order for every Catholic to embrace a life of mission. Someone once asked me how we can know that a parish has really been transformed and arrived where it needs to be in terms of building a culture of discipleship. In reality, the question is flawed. We are never really *there*; growth is always possible. The real goal for renewing parish culture is much bigger than we tend to realize. It should extend beyond disciple formation to create a cycle of fruitfulness that impacts the local community and spreads out beyond that to the whole world. To me, that is the final level of a culture of discipleship.

This is much bigger than getting parishioners plugged into ministries. Too often, our parishes do a poor job supporting and training lay leaders in evangelization. As leaders, at the end of the day, we want peo-

Building disciples means allowing space for the Holy Spirit to use their particular gifts and vision.

ple to just volunteer. We prefer to remain in control of things. This culture of volunteerism, where we ask people to devote their time and energy exclusively in support or administrative roles, is ultimately a barrier to authentic growth in mission. Building disciples means allowing space for the Holy Spirit to use their particular gifts and vision. It means giving them opportunities to feel the impetus toward this final phase: Send.

Do not be afraid of giving people actual agency in the work of evangelization at your parish, if they are well formed. Look at your parish right now. What are the various ways for leaders to get involved? Now ask yourself this question: How many opportunities for involvement have something to do with assisting at Mass on Sundays?

This is a subtle and deep problem in many of our parishes. The documents of the Second Vatican Council boldly proclaimed that lay people are called to be the salt of the earth, to explode out of the doors of Sunday Mass to re-Christify the world after receiving him into their very selves. This was supposed to lead to a deeper understanding and celebration of the role of the laity in the Church. Instead, what happened was what Saint John Paul II called a "clericalization of the laity" and a "laicization of the clergy."[43] Too often, clergy have become administrators and business managers alone, while lay people have been pulled into roles around the altar, instead of being pushed out into the world. Part of renewing our parish culture, then, is restoring the clergy and the laity to their proper roles. The clergy, through administering sacraments, preaching, and governance are called to sanctify the lay faithful so that the laity can go out and sanctify the world.

Pope Francis reiterates this point in his typically direct fashion: "We priests tend to clericalize the laity. We do not realize it, but it is as if we infect them with our own disease. And the laity — not all, but many — ask us on their knees to clericalize them, because it is more comfortable to be an altar server than the protagonist of a lay path."[44]

We are not done forming people once they are disciples, growing in their own personal relationship with Jesus. Each disciple is called is to become apostolic, to let their relationship with Jesus bear fruit in the lives of others. This is the call of each baptized Christian. The most spiritually healthy people are not just in Bible studies with others, they are on mission. The next chapter will discuss what Sending looks like in a parish.

ACTIVITY: Crafting a Parish Pathway

Follow the prompts below to start praying as a parish team about how you can build a discipleship pathway in your parish. These questions are based on the process through which L'Alto Catholic Institute takes individual parishes in our Parish Partnership.

WIN at your parish

Reflect:
1) Are there pre-evangelization outreaches at our parish currently that could be built up and used in our discipleship pathway?
2) Do we need to create a brand new pre-evangelization step?

Decide:
1) Our key pre-evangelization outreaches will be:

2)   Our preferred onboarding points for the pathway will be:

_____

_____

_____

_____

3)   Our WIN step, which will provide the opportunity to hear the Gospel preached and an invitation to individuals to give their lives to Christ, will be accomplished by implementing the following:

_____

_____

_____

_____

BUILD at your parish

Reflect:
1)   Are there any small groups at our parish that could be strengthened to help members grow in relationship with Christ and used in our pathway? What are those groups?
2)   Do we need to create a new "Build" process?

Decide:
1) Our prioritized "Build" process will be:

_____

_____

_____

_____

SEND at your parish

Reflect:
1) Are there any opportunities within our parish, pathway, or community that can be utilized in sending people on mission?
2) How will we prioritize the pathway as an opportunity for newly-formed missionary disciples to serve? What other outreaches will we promote?

Decide:
1) The SEND step at our parish will use the following formation to teach disciples to become missionary:

_____

_____

_____

_____

2) The SEND step at our parish will prioritize the following
    apostolic opportunities:

_____

_____

_____

_____

CHAPTER 7

The Third Key: Mobilize Leaders

"And what you heard from me before many witnesses entrust
to faithful men who will be able to teach others also."
— 2 Timothy 2:2

There are roughly 75 million registered Catholics in the United States and 17,500 parishes.[45] If every Catholic came to Mass every week (and, God willing, that will be the case someday), the average attendance at a U.S. parish would be about 4,000 people every week. Actual attendance numbers, according to a recent Gallup report, is about 40 percent.[46] That's still an average of 1,600 every week. The Hartford Institute defines a megachurch as any church that averages more than 2,000 people in weekly attendance.[47]

The conclusion: Our parishes are huge entities. This is one of the reasons why there is so much organizational dysfunction and burnout in the Church today, for both priests and laity. Having to work at such a massive scale means we often stop worrying about

The size and scale of many parishes makes culture change impossible for one person, or even a few people, to accomplish.

flourishing and become content with just functioning. The size and scale of many parishes makes culture change impossible for one person, or even a few people, to accomplish. If we want to change the culture of parishes to become dynamic centers of missionary discipleship, we have to get more leaders in the parish to join us in guiding the effort.

Recently, a friend wrote on his Facebook wall, "To my friends in ministry, if you saw your work at your parish as a year-long consulting gig, what would you do?" This question is a poignant one. We cannot work as though we will always be there to continue in our roles. If we do, the fruitfulness of our work ends when we do. If others can carry the torch after us, though, the effort can compound over time. This is why, as leaders, we need to spend as much time as possible with small groups of individuals, training them to carry on the vision after we are gone.

There is an all-too-common scenario that impacts our parishes today. A dynamic pastor or ministry leader arrives in a new role. They spend the first year just getting to understand the lay of the land. In year two, they start making small changes. Year three, they really start to push forward with their vision. By year five, real cultural change is just starting to happen. In year six, they are gone, either to a new parish or a new ministry role.

If culture change is going to be sustained in one parish over a long period of time, there needs to be a core group of "torchbearers" to carry the light of renewal through the long and difficult process. The stark reality is that real culture change takes ten years. It is a long-term process. We need leaders to be engaged in the process for that whole time, and that means we need to spend a lot of time upfront bringing a core group together and training people to lead.

This is the method of Jesus. During his public ministry, he had three years to accomplish the mission that the Father gave him. Granted, he spent plenty of time teaching large crowds and performing miracles, but the brunt of his efforts, his greatest "strategy," was to train twelve guys to carry the torch forward. Thousands of years later, people still need to hear the Gospel, and Christ needed someone to carry on the mission and make sure that we did.

The key and operative word for parish renewal is "resilient." We need to craft structures and initiatives that will be resilient as we push forward through the ups and downs that inevitably come with needed change. A steady leadership team can help beat the drum of discipleship in your parish long after the initial enthusiasm of something big, shiny, exciting, and new has worn off.

What should this structure of leadership look like? It must be resilient, avoid silos, and be able to bring about wide impact. To get there, we must imitate the leadership structure Jesus himself used. Jesus had plenty of followers. We do not know the exact number, but we know that at one point he fed a gathering that included 5,000 men, not counting the women and children. This means the total group was probably in the tens of thousands — the equivalent of filling an NBA arena.

We know from the Gospels that Jesus dedicated a large proportion of his time to forming smaller groups of individuals. He knew that long-term fruitfulness depends on others being able to stand in lockstep with his vision and carry it down through the centuries in foreign lands. Jesus organized his leaders this way:

JESUS

**Peter, James,
John**

The Twelve Apostles

The Seventy-Two (Luke 10)

I recommend that parishes visualize their leadership structure similarly, not in terms of exact numbers, but with a similar vision. Remember, as we begin this culture change, we are trying always to operate out of this paradigm:

vision → strategy → tactics

Burnout happens when one person or group takes on responsibility for each of the three levels. Having clearly defined priorities helps to buffer any one individual from having to shoulder the entire load him or herself. Here is a way to envision how this sharing of the load should take place in your parish:

Vision: Pastor
Strategy: Senior Leadership Team
Tactics: The "Seventy-Two"

PASTOR   VISION
                                  ↓
Leadership   STRATEGY
Team   ↓
Staff/Councils   TACTICS

Missionary Disciples

VISION: Pastor

The pastor has a crucial and irreplaceable role in leading the renewal of the parish. He is the key vision-caster. If the pastor is not pushing for change, total cultural renewal is next to impossible.

The first reason is practical and obvious: People look to the pastor for leadership. If an effort toward discipleship is happening without the pastor as the primary driver, it will be seen as a fringe movement within the parish. Yet what we are going for here is an entirely new vision for what it means to be a Catholic parish.

If the pastor is not pushing for change, total cultural renewal is next to impossible.

The second reason is spiritual: The authority given to the pastor as spiritual father of a parish is real and effective. The Church's hierarchical structure was not invented by some old guys in Rome during the Dark Ages; it was instituted by Christ. Those in positions of authority in the Church are given real spiritual authority, and God wants us to respect the authority they have by virtue of their office. For these reasons, I think the pastor should be an essential part of the cultural renewal of a parish.

Today, parish priests have to wear many hats. They preach and teach, celebrate the sacraments, visit hospitals, fundraise, and spiritually direct, all while administering a multimillion-dollar not-for-profit. Oh, yeah, and sometimes they run a school.

Gone are the days of a handful of priests living together in community and sharing these tasks. Not only is it common for a priest to be alone in running a parish, he is often given multiple parishes to run. I had a friend who became a priest and within eleven months of ordination, he was the pastor of four different parishes. The drive-time between the two outermost parishes was almost an hour.

In the face of this shifting role of the priest, many well-meaning Catholics have begun to argue that there should be more business classes in the seminary. This is misguided. Yes, on a practical level it does make sense: If Father had more business training, he would be able to lead his parish, with its various budgets and administrative demands, more effectively. It is also true that many priests are on fire for mission and service, but not at all motivated to be administrators, and this can lead to organizational dysfunction. Yet the reality is that these responsibilities should not fall solely on the priest. Surely, the staff accountant or a knowledgeable parishioner can help with the nuts and bolts of the business end of running a parish.

More than an MBA, a parish priest in the present age needs to be formed to be a *visionary leader*. In fact, we should be seeking ways to remove administrative responsibilities from our priests precisely so that parishes can become centers of evangelistic renewal. As a Church, if we are to carry out this vision for renewal, we do not need priests who are businessmen; we need priests who are leaders.

The hierarchical structure of the Church is inherent to who she is. Jesus knew what he was doing when he instituted the sacrament of Holy Orders, and one of the *munera* (offices) of Holy Orders is to govern. It is inherent to the vocation of the priesthood to *lead*. We need more priests who know how to live up to that lofty call.

Winston Churchill was not able to usher England through World War II just because he could run an effective meeting. Mahatma Gandhi did not inspire radical social change because he was a good fundraiser. Saint Joan of Arc was not able to lead armies the way she did because she was good at spreadsheets. Neither did any of these individuals do any of those things because they were perfect or without flaws. They led boldly because they were filled with conviction and vision and had the strength of character to make those visions come to life.

Times of crisis need visionaries, leaders who are willing to think differently and act courageously, reading the signs of the times. Meetings, fundraising, spreadsheets — all of these are an important part of leading an organization today, but more than anything, we need leaders who know how to cast vision. It begins with our priests, but this kind of visionary leadership is not reserved for pastors alone. Visionary leadership is accessible to all those whom God has called to a position of influence. While I want to hold up what I believe to be the essential role of the pastor in the spiritual leadership of the parish, I am not unaware that the importance I am placing there might make some lay staff and parish leaders uncomfortable. In the above paragraphs, I am trying to present the ideal scenario. In some situations, however, including ones I have encountered personally, the pastor is actually one of the main obstacles to the kind of renewal and cultural change this book is proposing, for a variety of reasons. What to do then? In those cases,

1) **Pray for a new outpouring of the Holy Spirit on your pastor:** God can help give your pastor a new vision. Maybe, if he is resistant to change, he really needs a renewal in his own heart, first.

2) **Go make disciples.** As we have said, real renewal comes from disciples being formed. You can do that on your own, in your homes. You do not need the permission of your pastor to live out the mission of the Church in your own life. Gather a group of like-minded individuals and get after it! Perhaps seeing your positive progress will encourage your pastor that your disciple-making ideas are good ones.

STRATEGY: Senior Leadership Team

Most of our priests are already operating at full capacity, so the pastor cannot go at it alone. Neither can he delegate the task to a committee and consider it done. Driving culture change is demanding, and it requires a multiplicity of gifts and visions.

Driving culture change is demanding, and it requires a multiplicity of gifts and visions.

It takes vulnerability, but leading cultural change will require a senior leadership team of a few committed individuals, working in concert with the pastor, who can be responsible for the strategic oversight of a renewal effort. I usually recommend five members for this team.

The senior leadership team is not responsible for running individual ministries but for overseeing strategy for all the parish's renewal efforts and for evaluating the fruitfulness (or not) of those efforts. This team is the glue to hold everything together, making sure the overall mission of the parish is being prioritized. They oversee and protect the clear path to discipleship and make sure that each strategic step of that pathway is actually accomplishing its mission. If not, they tweak what is being done or even give it up entirely. For more on pastors leading with a senior leadership team, look to the experts on the subject: the Amazing Parish movement at amazingparish.org.

Every leader attempting renewal needs a team. If you are leading a ministry in a parish, your number one priority should be gathering a team around you to do hands-on ministry with you. If you are in charge of anything at a parish, your very first job is to raise up other leaders to work alongside you. In this way, you multiply your impact. Youth ministry is the one area in most parishes where the idea of a "core team" is utilized effectively, but that model needs to be implemented in all ministries across parish life.

TACTICS: The "Seventy-Two"

The second phase of building a leadership structure involves forming the "seventy-two." I generally recommend to parish leadership that, at the beginning of a culture change effort, before any kind of launch weekend, they take a larger group off-site somewhere to form them in a vision for mission and evangelization. This group should be a mix of key staff, dedicated parishioners, and disciples who can catch fire for the renewal effort and be the torchbearers going forward, leading groups and programs, articulating the vision to others in the parish who might not understand, and praying in a dedicated way for renewal.

I love the way one pastor I encountered did this. He identified fifteen couples, families, and singles within his parish to form the "tip of the spear" for culture change efforts over the next decade. He and his director of evangelization then spent the entire first year of the renewal process just investing in these people. Together, they ran discipleship groups for them, took them on a retreat, and mentored them one-on-one. This pastor is a leader who understands that growth begins with investing in equipping and developing other leaders.

Raising up other leaders is not just about saying, "Hey, you! Lead." Remember, Jesus spent three years walking with his apostles. Then when Pentecost came around, they were sent out to grow the Church. That does not mean the apostles were not doing any ministry in the meantime, though. In fact, the Gospels record multiple instances of the apostles performing ministry while Jesus was still on earth. He walked with them that whole time to equip and develop them into leaders.

The healthiest parishes imitate Jesus in this. They do not just throw leaders out there to start doing ministry, but intentionally mentor them to do a specific thing. To those who are already intentional disciples, "faithful men," as the quote from 2 Timothy at the outset of this chapter put it, they hand a specific mission and then form them specifically to accomplish that mission effectively. A real missional role in a parish should challenge, push, and stretch a faithful person. It should push them beyond their capacity, requiring real growth. At the same time, other leaders must walk with individual leaders as they are being stretched in order to support and guide that growth.

This is especially true of young people in positions of leadership within a parish. Many Millennials I have talked to, in particular, crave this kind of equipping. They do not just want to be plugged in to a spot that needs a volunteer. They want to be raised up by others in leadership to accomplish a vitally important mission for the fruitfulness of the parish. They want to be doing something that is integral to the overall mission of the parish to form disciples.

Dying that they might live

"Unless a grain of wheat falls into the earth, it remains alone; but if it dies, it bears much fruit."

— John 12:24

Before we can give others a new vision, we ourselves need to be given a new heart by God. If we are to invite renewal into the lives of those whom we serve, then we first need to be renewed ourselves in the Holy Spirit. This renewal only happens in the wilderness.

Think of the greatest innovators and reformers in the Church. In every age of the Church, God has raised up great saints who have a simple and clear vision of what they need to do in order to be witnesses to the Gospel. These saints have followed their calling and invited others to take part in it. Here are just a few examples:

- While traveling by train from Calcutta to Darjeeling, Mother Teresa heard God speak to her. This was her famous "call within a call" to "quench the infinite thirst of Jesus on the cross for love and souls" by "laboring at the salvation and sanctification of the poorest of the poor."[48]

- Saint Ignatius of Loyola, with a simple desire to assemble an army of missionaries for God, formed the Society of Jesus as a place where any could serve who desired to live as a "soldier of God."

- Saint Francis de Sales felt an urgent call to bring the Calvinists in his area back to the Catholic Church. For three years, he trudged around snowy Switzerland, handing out pamphlets on the Faith. He ultimately was responsible for converting 40,000 back to the Catholic Faith.

In each case, the saint heard a simple call from God and then patiently and almost stubbornly responded. They executed upon their vision even in the midst of incredible trials and obstacles.

For our work in parishes, the example of these saints shows that we must begin with becoming the kind of person God can work through. And this involves a lot of surrender. Before we can cast vision and lead culture change in our parishes, we have to be able to surrender our own plans and vision and even our desire for the esteem of others. Before we build an evangelizing parish, we have to lay our vision before God and make sure that it is a God-given one.

> *Before we build an evangelizing parish, we have to lay our vision before God and make sure that it is a God-given one.*

The best way to start casting vision as a leader of renewal is to ask the Lord what he desires for your community. What is God's dream for your parish in this time? This is the logic, not of corporate America, but of the saints: They receive their mission and vision more than they create it.

The greatest obstacle to casting vision for our parishes is our own pride, our own desire to be liked, respected, and revered. The Litany of Humility is the greatest leadership tool we have. We also have to be willing, not just to lay our vision at the feet of Jesus, but also to surrender our own desire for success. It is a natural human desire to want to be successful; it is a supernatural desire to want to see the Kingdom built.

If we want true success as leaders in our parishes, we have to be willing to be led into the wilderness by God, to have our own hearts shaped, forged, and even broken. It is only once our hearts are cracked open by God that he can begin to work his vision through us. As Michael O'Brien writes in his book *The Father's Tale,* "The only whole heart is a broken one."

It is probably no coincidence that Mother Teresa did the amazing work she did while suffering in spiritual darkness for almost fifty years. This is how Christianity has always worked. We follow a God whose method of success and victory is the Cross. Our path as leaders, if it is to be about authentic renewal, will be an invitation to similar degradation.

The friends of Jesus Christ are willing to enter into the darkness with him, to be broken down themselves, so that renewal can be brought about. Leading renewal cannot be about our own self-exaltation, about other people seeing the work we are accomplishing and recognizing how holy and talented we are. Leading change is about giving up our desire to be applauded and committing to entering into the spiritual path of renewal that God has for us so he can forge us in his image, and so that we can bring life to others. As Saint Catherine of Siena put it, "Become who you are and you will set the world on fire."

Start a movement
Forming leaders is about more than just finding functionaries to operate different parish-based ministries. One of the best things we can do with the Seventy-Two is to mobilize them to disciple others in the context of small groups with one-on-one investment.

Here is a true story of the kind of impact one disciple can have in a parish. I have a friend who, upon moving to a new parish with his wife and small children, discerned a calling to reach out to other young couples in the parish who might not yet have truly encountered Christ. After Mass each Sunday, this couple would find another couple they had not seen before, approach them, and introduce themselves. "Hey, we're new to the parish and we don't know many people yet. We were wondering if you wanted to join our family for brunch this morning."

They developed a few friendships this way, and then they began hosting a Bible study with a few of these couples in their house after Mass every Sunday. About a year and a half after this group was formed, the fruits were already enormously apparent. The participants had made great new friends, and many of them who had been semi-committed Catholics before were growing closer to Christ by the day. It turned out that several of the members of the group were not actually Catholic when the group was formed. They were simply joining their spouse for Mass on Sundays. By the end of the year and a half, three members of the group had gone through RCIA to become Catholics. Our friend began forming another couple in the group to take over leadership of the Bible study so that he could begin a new one.

This extraordinary fruit came from one couple's simple efforts: they sought first to make friends, then to build community, and from those efforts disciples were formed. Properly done, this is simply the most effective and personal way to reach a pivotal number of people. If you engage disciples who form disciples who themselves are capable of forming disciples, an unstoppable movement will be started that will radically transform your parish's culture over time. It begins by simply following the Holy Spirit's promptings and reaching out to one or two people at a time. If we are faithful, the Lord multiplies our efforts exponentially.

Jesus came to fulfill the mission he had received from his Father to bring the whole world back into a relationship with God (cf. Jn 3:16), if they choose to accept that gift of salvation. He is the universal Savior because God wills that all should be saved, and there is no salvation except in Jesus Christ.[49]

While Jesus' mission is universal, it is interesting to note that during his earthly ministry, Jesus remained pretty ... lo-

cal. Why did he stay primarily in the small geographic boundaries of the Holy Land? Furthermore, even while staying local,
why did he spend so much time with twelve, uneducated, ordinary guys?

The reason is simple: Evangelization is not about complicated formulas, it is about relationships. There is an inherent inefficiency to really effective evangelization because it
is based on this kind of intentional relationship-building in
order to help guide others into transformative relationship
with God. Jesus knew that when he ascended to the Father, his
apostles would carry on his mission for him. The founding of
a Church that would be the sacred sign of himself to the whole
world would depend on these distinctly human vessels. So he
walked with them.

*Jesus believed in the process
of spiritual multiplication, and
if it was his strategy, it should
be ours too.*

Jesus believed in the process
of spiritual multiplication, and
if it was his strategy, it should
be ours too. The simple math of
spiritual multiplication is that
the most effective method of evangelization is not just to form
disciples, but to form disciples capable of making disciples,
creating exponential growth. This is not a multilevel marketing scheme, but about genuinely loving people. This kind of
walking with people one at a time is about valuing individuals
and addressing their needs in the context of real relationship.
It is not an attempt to mass produce discipleship.

An important part of pushing for culture change in our
parishes is to begin this kind of multiplying movement, investing in a handful of people who can then go do the same
for others. This way of growth can make a significant impact
on your parish in the long term.

CHAPTER 8

The Fourth Key: Align Everything

Segmentation is, for good or ill, very common in parishes, which means many parish initiatives operate in silos. Everything has its own bucket with its own staff person in charge, budget, and volunteers. Because this is the way parishes operate, it can be far too easy to turn evangelization into just another parish silo. If your goal is real cultural change, this mentality needs to shift at every level of the parish.

When we are talking about making a cultural change to craft parishes as hubs of evangelization and discipleship, we are talking about seeing everything we do in a new way. If our overall parish has been stuck in maintenance mode, then most of the individual ministries will have a business-as-usual way of doing things and will need help getting unstuck. We cannot let any aspect of church life in our parish remain in maintenance mode.

As we begin to cast vision, develop a clear path to discipleship, and mobilize leaders, we also need to be ensuring that everything we do as a parish aligns with this more missional vision. Earlier, at the end of chapter one, we mentioned how George Weigel gives a helpful paradigm for renewing anything in the Church in this era of the New Evangeliza-

tion. When we are trying to reform any aspect of parish life
and ministry, we must first ask
Authentic renewal never what the thing is so that we can
changes the core of what rearticulate the truth of what it
something is, but it does make is in light of mission. Authentic
sure that it prioritizes mission. renewal never changes the core
of what something is, but it does
make sure that it prioritizes mission.

In most parishes, there are four important areas of ministry that must be aligned with a more evangelizing vision. They are:

1) Sacramental preparation
2) Religious education
3) Communications
4) Major liturgical holy days (Christmas, Ash Wednesday, Easter)

SACRAMENTAL PREPARATION

After my conversion when I was eighteen, I began to develop an incredible love for the Eucharist. This reality that Jesus was so near at Mass and in adoration was a deep comfort and formed the center of my devotional life. I was really blown away by how close God wants to come to us.

As the doctrine of the Real Presence settled in my mind, however, I could not shake a strange feeling I had. I looked back on my own life, and I realized I had received Communion many times without really being changed. Now that I was becoming more aware of Christ's presence in the Eucharist, it seemed strange to me that the power of Jesus present in the Eucharist, which I was now watching erode my selfishness and open my heart to greater love of God, had been so lacking in impact for so many years.

Thankfully, I did not have to wait long for an answer. One of my first theology classes in college included a lengthy study of sacramental theology. We were forced to memorize section 1131 of the *Catechism*, which provides an excellent, brief summary of the sacraments. Thanks to that professor, I can still recite this section by memory. The last line, in particular, is key for those of us involved in parish renewal and evangelization:

> The sacraments are efficacious signs of grace, instituted by Christ and entrusted to the Church, by which divine life is dispensed to us. The visible rites by which the sacraments are celebrated signify and make present the graces proper to each sacrament. *They bear fruit in those who receive them with the required dispositions* (emphasis added).

The efficacy of the entire sacramental economy around which the Church is organized depends on our spiritual disposition as recipients. In other words, the sacraments can only bear fruit in our lives if we let them. The all-powerful God of the universe sets up a plan for our salvation that runs directly through these seven sacraments, and they can only "work" fully in our lives when we say yes.

The scary reality here is that much of the grace being offered in these incredible, privileged encounters with God, is not effective in many of the people who participate in them. In Matthew 13, Jesus goes back to his hometown, Nazareth, and is not received well. The story ends with a chilling line: "And he did not do many mighty works there, because of their unbelief" (Mt 13:58). The same principle applies to the sacraments. Where the objective grace of the sacraments encounters the obstacles of unbelief and lack of openness, the grace is not subjectively effective.

This is true, not just of the Eucharist, but all the sacraments. Baptism and Confirmation are often treated as mere rites of passage; we receive the Eucharist as "that thing you do" at Mass; and Confession becomes relegated to people who actually have a sense of the workings of grace. In other words, God gives us the ability to limit his power when we say no to his grace.

Often enough, parishes do not act like this is really true. Too often, we operate like sacrament vending machines. In sacramental preparation and afterward, more work has to be done to elicit the faith that lets God work wonders through the sacramental economy.

Too often, we operate like sacrament vending machines. In sacramental preparation and afterward, more work has to be done to elicit the faith that lets God work wonders through the sacramental economy.

We do not reflect enough on this incredible truth in our parishes. Instead, we sometimes treat the sacraments like magic, like our role as parishes is to just put our parishioners through the Catholic sacramental car wash. In reality, although most parish leaders realize that this is an ineffective way of forming disciples, they just do not know what to do to change it. In our work to transform the culture of our parishes, sacramental preparation should be a key area of our focus. Turning sacramental prep into a truly evangelizing process is crucial, not only for parish renewal, but for the efficacy of the sacraments themselves. God wants to work wonders through his sacraments and we have to do our part to prepare people for that.

Marriage prep

In our current cultural moment, marriage preparation has become a key piece of the evangelization puzzle. It is no secret that a great many people who present themselves for the Sacrament of Matrimony in the Church are not practicing the Faith. Many have been away from the Church for a long time, having left in college or young adulthood. Many times, they are only coming back to be married in the Church because someone else in their family (such as parents or grandparents) wants them to.

Archbishop Allen Vigneron of the Archdiocese of Detroit released an incredibly valuable pastoral letter in 2017, urging a return to evangelization. The letter, entitled "Unleash the Gospel," calls for marriage preparation to become a kind of "second catechumenate."[50] We should utilize marriage prep to welcome couples who have not been practicing the Faith back into parish life. Since a relationship with Jesus is the most important thing for a healthy marriage, we should make intentionally evangelizing moments a key part of marriage prep.

We should utilize marriage prep to welcome couples who have not been practicing the Faith back into parish life.

One priest friend of mine stands out as a strong witness of what this kind of marriage prep can look like. He has personally prepared hundreds of couples for marriage. Aware of the faith situation of many of those who come to him for help preparing for marriage, he knew that something different needed to be done. He committed to building a relationship with each couple over the months of their engagement. Each session would last anywhere from two to four hours. He and the couple would share a meal, and he would teach. They would go over the results of a standard but extensive marriage preparation questionnaire and use that as a launching point for their conversation, but he would also tell a sweeping narrative of the story of salvation history and where marriage fits into it, drawing heavily on Saint John Paul II's *Theology of the Body.* This priest would build a relationship with the couple before speaking to them about the teachings and rules that are most challenging. As a result, he was even often successful getting couples who were living together before marriage to stop cohabitating. He told me that out of the hundreds of couples he had prepared for marriage, only one had ever been divorced, and it was a family member.

I know another parish that equips and develops young couples in the parish to mentor and build friendships with couples going through marriage preparation, using very similar tactics as those my priest friend employs. The parish has seen great success with this. They include a retreat for all of the couples and mentor couples at a retreat center nearby, making it not just a powerful spiritual experience but also an engaging social event with wine, bourbon, and meals.

This is a time intensive process, to be sure, but evangelization always is. Just getting people through the sacramental pipeline is easy. Investing deeply in friendships so that people can meet Jesus is much more costly to our own time and energy. The question is: Is it worth it to us as a parish?

For Reflection
- How can we approach sacramental preparation at our parish with an emphasis on evangelizing those seeking the sacraments?
- In what ways could we incorporate our Discipleship Pathway?
- What unique considerations might we have for these individuals as we strive to win, build, and send them?

RCIA

In a positive move, many Rite of Christian Initiation for Adults (RCIA) programs now do a good job of teaching the *Didache* or catechesis. As parishes, we need to invest further in making RCIA, particularly inquiry, a specifically evangelistic and pre-evangelistic process.

When most people present themselves to begin the process of RCIA, they are not already disciples. The rite itself anticipates that fact and indicates that the period of inquiry (or the pre-catechumenate) is specifically set aside for evangelization leading to an initial conversion, with significant attention given to the preaching of the Gospel. One reason some new Catholics fall away again when RCIA is over is because parishes become so attached to their process, rather than worrying about fruitfulness or the outcome. Sadly, we have generally not devoted enough time to making sure that evangelization is primary.

Here are some initiatives I have seen in different parishes that provide useful structures for developing a more evangelizing intent with the RCIA:

- Instituting a year-round catechumenate;
- Providing more fully developed mystagogy that includes substantial spiritual formation;
- Building personal relationships between parishioners and candidates/catechumens through mentoring relationships and involvement in small groups with people outside of RCIA;
- Bringing in programs like Alpha or ChristLife as a key piece of the inquiry process; and
- Holding an evangelizing retreat.

RITE OF CHRISTIAN INITIATION OF ADULTS

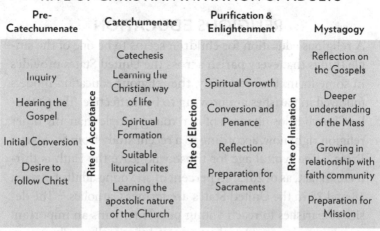

Pre-Catechumenate		Catechumenate		Purification & Enlightenment		Mystagogy
Inquiry	Rite of Acceptance	Catechesis	Rite of Election	Spiritual Growth	Rite of Initiation	Reflection on the Gospels
Hearing the Gospel		Learning the Christian way of life		Conversion and Penance		Deeper understanding of the Mass
Initial Conversion		Spiritual Formation		Reflection		Growing in relationship with faith community
Desire to follow Christ		Suitable liturgical rites		Preparation for Sacraments		
		Learning the apostolic nature of the Church				Preparation for Mission

As with all things, it is less about what you do and more about how you do it. Just tweaking our RCIA structures alone will not necessarily lead to the fruit that we want. At the end of the day, we know that some combination of preaching the Gospel, genuine friendships, and prayer lead to fruitfulness.

For Reflection

- How could our WIN step be a part of the Evangelization and Pre-Catechumenate phase? What additional formation/support may we need to provide specifically to those pursuing RCIA?
- What would it look like to integrate our Build step into these phases of RCIA? What unique considerations and additional formation might we need to have for those in RCIA in the Build step?
- How could we provide formation for sponsors (and all those involved in RCIA) to help them in their own journey as disciples, as well as how they can share that vision with the catechumens?
- What special consideration may we need for those who have just received sacraments at Easter? How could we teach a reliance on the Holy Spirit?

RELIGIOUS EDUCATION

A religious education for children seems to be one of the single things that every parish across the United States provides in some form. Unfortunately, the religious education models followed in parishes are proving to be ineffective. The Catholic Church is losing more of her young people than any other religion right now, according to a recent study from St. Mary's Press.[51] The typical age for those who leave the Faith is thirteen. In fact, as of 2015, 13 percent of all young adults between 18 and 25 in the United States are former Catholics.[52] The desire of parishes to reach young people remains an important one, but we have yet to adopt a model that really works.

A study done in 2012 in Canada, called "Hemorrhaging Faith," looked into the factors that led to young people retaining their faith through young adulthood as opposed to walking away. The study identified four factors that make the most substantial difference for young people who do *not* leave their faith. These young people:

1) Have experienced God's presence and seen answered prayer;
2) Can ask and openly discuss their real spiritual questions in the Christian community;
3) Understand the Gospel (kerygma) at a deep level; and
4) Have seen communities of faith and older adults authentically live their faith.

Religious education models can certainly be adapted to focus on these four elements, but most are not currently set up to do so. It could even be said that many parishes might actually be more successful at forming young people in the Faith if they dropped all religious education programming completely and *We cannot stress enough how important it is to provide consistent ongoing formation for adults in our parishes.* just focused on adult evangelization. While this is somewhat hyperbolic, we cannot stress enough how important it is to provide consistent ongoing formation for adults in our parishes. This is good, not only for the adults themselves, but for the children as well. The very best thing we can do for the discipleship of the children in our parish is to deepen the faith of their parents. For this reason, it is encouraging to see many parishes commit to family faith formation models that include formation for the parents, helping them retain their role as primary educators in the Faith.

For Reflection

- What does religious education/sacramental preparation look like currently at our parish?
- What is working well?
- What hasn't worked well?
- In what ways are we currently trying to reach parents/entire families who are not yet disciples?

COMMUNICATIONS

To communicate the Gospel to other people is at the heart of evangelization. There is a certain sense in which communication is the fundamental purpose of the Church. Saint Paul says, "Faith comes from what is heard" (Rom 10:17). As a parish seeking to become more missionally oriented, we must refocus the way we communicate. This means taking a serious look at three factors: who, how, and why. To whom we are trying to communicate? How we do so? And why do we communicate at all?

With Whom Are You Communicating?

Reading the average parish website, bulletin, and weekly announcements (the key ways most parishes communicate with people) reveals a lot of insider language that is completely inaccessible to outsiders. Wall Street has its own "insider lingo" that can be difficult to comprehend for those less experienced in that subculture. Just watch CNBC and try to make sense of half the words their anchors use. Parishes can be the same way.

Consider this example: "If you would like to join RCIA, please drop off a form in the parish office." We have all heard this or a similar announcement at our parish or parishes we have visited. Innocuous as it may sound, this statement has a lot of problems. Here are some of the most critical issues:

1) This announcement assumes people — especially those people who most need RCIA — already

know what RCIA is, which is often not true. There is no explanation of the program, nor does it even provide an explanation of what the four letters stand for.

2) This announcement also assumes the people who most need RCIA are aware that they need it. It provides no indicators of why RCIA is important and necessary. (It also assumes that they are actually in attendance at the Mass!)

3) Finally, this announcement places the burden on the potential attendee. In order to join RCIA, they are going to have to print off a form, fill it out, and bring it to the parish office during office hours. Note well that office hours in a typical parish are Monday through Friday between 9:00 a.m. and 4:00 p.m., when most other people are at work.

Looking at all three of these issues, it is clear that this announcement does not speak to the target audience. And this is just one example. Across our ministries and initiatives, parishes seeking to become more missionally oriented must seek to reach the disengaged, the fallen away, and the nonbeliever. That does not mean we do not challenge or call them deeper, but it does mean we need to be aware of the messages we send.

Across our ministries and initiatives, parishes seeking to become more missionally oriented must seek to reach the disengaged, the fallen away, and the non-believer.

In fact, I think it should sharpen our communication efforts in seeking to inspire.

The first step to making communications more mission focused is to make the disengaged, the fallen away, and the outsider the primary intended audience of most of your parish's communications. Your insiders will understand (after you help them see why it is important to do so), and you will help them to spend more time and energy thinking about those demographics as well.

How Are You Trying to Communicate with Them?

I once worked with a parish that was frustrated over their annual community picnic. They really wanted new people to come, but for multiple years, they had seen fewer and fewer new faces at the picnic and did not know what to do. I knew that the town had a really vibrant downtown area with tons of restaurants and bars. I asked if they had ever considered doing the event near that downtown area on a summer evening to attract people as they walked by. Maybe new people just were not comfortable coming to the Catholic church's parking lot for an event. They told me they had not considered that.

Did they mail out beautifully designed and engaging invitations to people's houses? The answer was no.

Did they knock on people's doors to let them know when the event was and that they would love to see them there? No, again.

If we want different results, we have to be willing to do things differently. If we want to reach people other than our "regulars," we have to communicate using different techniques. The question for us is, are we zealous enough for souls that we are willing to attempt to communicate with those outside of our parish community in a way that is accessible and invitational?

What works as far as communications tactics will vary depending on your circumstances but aligning your communication efforts with a more missional vision means identifying a target audience and then strategizing carefully about how you will reach them. The tactics should flow from the question of what is going to reach the people with whom you are trying to communicate.

Why Are You Communicating with Them?

Think about why your parish communicates what it does. What is the reason behind your bulletin announcements, pulpit announcements, and flyers? Often, the "why" is simply this: "So that people will come to the things we do."

This clearly falls short of our goal if we are serious about mission.

Parishes tend to be far too functional in their communication, rather than seeking to stir people's hearts. Not everything we communicate has to be a direct invitation to an event. Yes, our communication should always include some "call to action," but the call to action should not always be parish-centric. When that happens, we come across looking a little self-centered. Think about those friends you have on Facebook or Instagram who only ever promote their business or talk about themselves. It gets a little annoying, right? Yet too many parishes communicate this way. If our Why as parishes is to bring everyone into a relationship with Jesus Christ, then our communications need to tell people more about Jesus in a way that is attractive and engages the mind and heart.

Not everything we communicate has to be a direct invitation to an event.

A Note on Technology for the Kingdom

Technology has made for a busier, noisier, and more distracted world, yes, but it also gives parishes an opportunity. Using technology well, we are able to communicate the Gospel like never before. The parish's new front door is its website. Parish leaders should take note of this: a recent study by Forbes showed that 90 percent of people read online reviews before visiting a new business.[53] A full two-thirds said that they trust online search as the most trusted source of information on people and companies. If that is true of businesses, it is also likely true of your parish. How does that change the way you think about your web presence?

It is not hard to make a parish website simple, clean, visually appealing, and easy to use, with the most important information prominently exposed. A parish I used to work for had 3,000 registered families and averaged around 3,000 unique visitors to its website every month. That is an enormous amount of activity and needs to be leveraged for evangelization. We could go through every possible communication medium (Facebook, email, etc.) and talk about how to optimize them for mission, but that is not really our point here. The simple point is that if we are not leveraging current technology in effective ways, we are missing a huge opportunity our culture has placed in front of us to reach people.

Chances are you have within your parish social media experts, marketing experts, photographers, graphic designers, and others who can help you begin to create beautiful media that your Church can share. They simply have to be invited to put their gift at the service of your parish. At the same time, do not be afraid to pay them. Many parishes struggle to invest in communications, not seeing the value. This is a big mistake. If we are investing millions of dollars in our facilities because we want people to encounter something beautiful and feel welcomed, then we can invest thousands into crafting a beautiful web presence that has the same effect and invites people to try us out for the first time.

In an age of noise, attention is the great currency of our economy. Where companies once spent ad dollars on traditional marketing methods like billboards or TV commercials, today they are pumping money into people with large social media followings in specific niches to market and promote their products. These people are called social media influencers. In 2019, 6.5 billion dollars was spent on influencer-based marketing.[54] If we want to align our communications efforts with an overall parish vision for mission, then we need to make an effort at doing utilizing media excellently. We need to be as motivated to reach people through technology and social media as these companies are to sell their products.

Questions to ask as you plan your parish's social media use:

1) Whom do you want to reach?
2) Why are you communicating with them?
3) How will you reach them?
4) What will be the content of your message?

MAJOR LITURGICAL HOLY DAYS

There are enough remnants of cultural Catholicism in our society that many nominal Catholics will attend Mass on major liturgical holy days, especially Christmas, Easter, and (interestingly enough) Ash Wednesday. As a result, these Masses remain a crucial evangelistic opportunity. In a missional parish, these major liturgical holy days become prime occasions to reach a group of people who are often out of our reach. Sadly, many parishes miss out on this critical opportunity.

When we are visiting my in-laws in upstate New York, we will often go to my wife's childhood parish for Mass. It would be kind to say that attendance is pretty sparse at this parish. According to the Barna Group, that area in New York, upstate, is now one of the most secularized parts of the country,[55] and it shows. My in-laws' church is a massive, beautiful Gothic church, and on an average Sunday there are (at most) a couple hundred people at Mass. The seating capacity is at least two and a half times that number.

Imagine my shock, then, when we went to Midnight Mass at Christmas one year and could not find seats a full half-hour before Mass began. It was packed! I have never seen such a striking difference between a normal Sunday Mass and a big liturgical holy day. I waited to see what this parish would do to reach this flood of new people and invite them to more regular participation.

But the parish did nothing.

They had been given an incredible chance to tell a packed house about how all of their suffering, sin, emptiness, and brokenness, all the ways in which the world had promised them joy in walking away from Jesus and had failed to make good on that promise, could be found redeemed in the newborn Christ child. I wanted the homilist to shout about the goodness of Jesus Christ he had experienced in his own life and to implore the people filling the church to find the same joy he had discovered. I wanted people to walk out of that Christmas Eve Mass with their hearts burning for more. I wanted them to feel welcomed and loved. I was disappointed. This parish had the chance to invite people to give their entire hearts to Jesus, and they dropped the ball.

As we seek to become more mission-oriented, we should not miss out on these key liturgical holy days. Turn to the appendix for some practical suggestions to make these holy days an opportunity to reach people and invite them into a fulfilling relationship with Jesus.

For Reflection

- How do we currently try and reach newcomers at Christmas and Easter?
- What is our follow-up?
- Do we know what the "return rate" to following Masses might be?
- What has worked well?
- What hasn't worked?
- What are some other "out of the box" ideas we could use to engage people who come to us on major holy days?
- How can we approach on-ramps such as Christmas and Easter with a greater sense for evangelization?
- What would a "Come and See" event look like at our parish?

NEW WINESKINS

To align everything we do as a parish with a more missional, disciple-oriented vision requires that we attempt to live out Jesus' teaching in Matthew 9:16: "And no one puts a piece of unshrunk cloth on an old garment, for the patch tears away from the garment, and a worse tear is made."

If we are really serious about seeing cultural change at our parishes, then we need to rally everything we do around a vision for forming disciples. Making disciples is the unshrunk cloth and many of the "ways we have always done things" are, bluntly, an old garment. The whole thing has to be made new.

Evangelization and discipleship cannot be relegated to one program or one ministry, operating independently. Everything we do as a parish needs to come to serve that mission, which often means taking a serious look at many of our existing structures and reevaluating them in light of this missional call. This vision for the New Evangelization, for reestablishing the core of our faith, should permeate everything we do.

Evangelization and discipleship cannot be relegated to one program or one ministry, operating independently.

CONCLUSION

Responding to Our Cultural Moment

Jesus Christ said that the gates of hell will never prevail against the Church, but he did not say that she would not dwindle down in certain areas of the world. Even while she booms in certain parts of the world today, the Catholic Church in the West, due to advancing secularization and our own failures, is facing the very real and present danger of diminishing almost completely.

Pope Emeritus Benedict XVI, when he was a young priest, famously predicted:

> From the crisis of today the Church of tomorrow will emerge — a Church that has lost much. She will become small and will have to start afresh more or less from the beginning. She will no longer be able to inhabit many of the edifices she built in prosperity. As the number of her adherents diminishes, so it will lose many of her social privileges. In contrast to an earlier age, it will be seen much more as a voluntary society, entered only by free decision. As a small society, it will make much bigger demands on the initiative of her individual members.[56]

Some refer to this as the former pope's vision for the Church as a "creative minority." Even if this is the future of the Church in the United States, I believe we can and should work for renewal now, before we hit the demographic cliff that will see us become such a minority. Creative? Always. Minority? God willing, hopefully not! Maybe it is not too late to turn back the trend. Yet even if it is too late for that, and the Church is indeed destined to become a "creative minority," a significant cultural shift toward mission needs to happen in our parishes and in our hearts so that we will be equipped to reevangelize our culture.

The religious historian Phyllis Tickle is credited with the theory that Christianity has undergone a crisis about every five hundred years in its two-thousand-year history.[57] It seems to me that this is true, but I would take it further. Every age of crisis for the Church has also seen the rise of great saints and religious movements that helped restore the Church and led her into a period of fresh growth and renewed focus. Here is a basic timeline:

- First, the fall of the Roman Empire (around A.D. 476) and the ongoing debate surrounding the Christological heresies threw the Church into a period of crisis. The Church had become too comfortable as the official religion of the Roman Empire, and many of those in leadership within the Church were actual heretics. In the face of this grave state of affairs, the Church in the West witnessed the rise of the monastic movement, led by Saint Benedict. He gathered a community of monks around a life of prayer and work, centered in a monastic community. Benedict's sister, Saint Scholastica, formed a similar community of women, and these communities would not only preserve Catholic life and culture, but would become

incredible centers of learning that would eventually build an even greater society in the West. Hundreds of years later, many medieval towns were
completely built around those monasteries.

- By the time of the Great Schism in 1054, some
  of the monasteries had become corrupt, more
  focused on worldly pleasures and status than on
  humble simplicity for the sake of the Gospel. The
  Schism, which divided the Church of the West
  from the Church of the East, represented the first
  large scale splintering in Christian unity.

- In the twelfth century, Saints Francis and Clare of
  Assisi, along with Saint Dominic, would become
  the founders of some of the greatest religious orders the Church had ever seen. The mendicant
  Friars Minor and the Order of Preachers, known
  today as the Franciscans and Dominicans, together helped lead the charge for a true revitalization
  of the Church.

- On October 31, 1517, just over five hundred years
  ago, Martin Luther nailed his Ninety-Five The-
  ses to the door of the Wittenberg Castle church.
  Luther was an Augustinian monk, frustrated by
  some of the Church's doctrine and practice. With
  the help of the German landed nobility, he threw
  the Church into a crisis of splintering, the wounds
  of which are still felt today. The disillusionment
  wrought by the splintering of Christendom, along
  with the subsequent bloody wars fought between
  Protestants and Catholics, would be disillusioning
  for many. Yet on the heels of this great tragedy, the
  Church experienced a flowering of holiness. Saints

Teresa of Avila and John of the Cross led a refor-
mation of the Carmelite order, calling them to a
more rigorous following of their vows. Additionally, their writings laid out a roadmap for souls seeking transforming union with the Lord. Their writings remain an encouragement to lay and religious
alike to seek the heights of holiness. Saint Francis
de Sales personally led evangelistic expeditions in
once Catholic areas, bringing thousands back to
the Faith. His spiritual classic, *An Introduction to
the Devout Life*, trumpeted a universal call to holiness that still breathes life into the hearts of many.
Around this same time, the world was changed
forever by the discovery of the New World. Over
time, millions would be converted, following the
apparition of Our Lady of Guadalupe to Saint Juan
Diego near modern-day Mexico City. And also
during this time, Franciscan and Jesuit missionaries led incredible evangelistic missions through
much of the New World.

- Now we come to our present day. As we know all
too well, the Church today faces a present and
clear crisis. What is unique to our era, what best
summarizes our current difficulty, is secularization and the widespread abandonment of religious
belief and practice in once Christian societies.
This has not occurred overnight. In the nineteenth
century, the most influential philosopher of our
cultural era, Friedrich Nietzsche, triumphantly
proclaimed, "God is dead, and we killed him."[58]
The last vestiges of once-mighty Christendom are
officially gone. We officially live in a post-Christian culture. This moment, for the once Christian
West, is unlike any time that has come before. It is

true that no time has been perfect, because sin always exists in the human heart, but no other time
has seen secularization at the scale we are seeing
today. Multiple studies have shown that the most
quickly growing religious designation is "none."
This means that people, when asked, state that
they have no religious affiliation at all. Within
that designation, there is a spectrum from militant
atheist to soft agnostic, or even those who describe
themselves as "spiritual but not religious."

In each moment of cultural crisis, the renewal of the Church
and society has been brought about by the arising of a new,
creative, dynamic expression of Christian holiness. Histori-
cally, this has been found in the birth of new religious orders:
the Benedictines, the Franciscans and Dominicans, the Jesu-
its. I believe that in our moment, however, renewal will not
be led by religious orders, but by the laity. Since the Second
Vatican Council, the clarion call from the Holy Spirit has been
that it is the laity who are being called to lead the charge.

To get a sense of what this renewal must look like, we can
turn back to the religious orders that sprang up in response
to crises in the Church. Each of these dynamic expressions of
Christian life that led to renewal shared three common elements:

1) Radical commitment to holiness through prayer
    and asceticism;
2) Authentic community centered around love of
    God and love of neighbor; and
3) Desire to build the kingdom of God through
    self-sacrificial mission.

If our society today is to see renewal, if our Church is to be re-
built, it will be because the laity begin to live these three values

in creative and radical ways and, in my opinion, parishes have to lead the charge in this renewal. The normal parish experience has to be one that forms and sends this kind of Spirit-led lay person. What would our Church and our world look like if this kind of radical lay Catholicism were normative lay Catholicism?

In our parishes, we must form lay Catholics to be Gospel-oriented disciples. For too long, we have accepted the half-measures of membership and maintenance as "good enough." In our present era, with the current challenges and opportunities in front of us, we must be ready to do more. As leaders in parishes, we have a decision to make: We can either let our parish communities become places where this New Laity is supported, encouraged, and empowered, or we can keep it business-as-usual and manage our decline over the next couple generations.

My hope is that you have picked up this book because you have been craving this kind of renewal. You are not content with the average experience at your parish and you possess a burning hope that real renewal is possible and that our Church, the Bride of Christ, can once again bring many souls to him.

This renewal will take time, because it is a renewal of hearts. There is no doubt that we live in interesting times with shifting cultural sands. It is no accident that God has chosen us for these times, and my conviction is that if we each commit to tilling the soil that is in front of us, if we focus our efforts on building up the local and domestic churches in which we are placed, we will see the new springtime that Saint John Paul II prophesied.

Resources for Culture Change

This list of resources is far from exhaustive, but the ministries recommended here are some of the best I know to help parishes form missionary disciples. I should also note that while I offer many programmatic suggestions here, every program is, at the end of the day, just a tool and not an end in itself. Tools can be used effectively or ineffectively; it depends on if they are being led by Spirit-led leaders or not. A Google search will find you more information and websites for any of these outreaches.

- **L'Alto Catholic Institute:** L'Alto Catholic Institute is the organization I lead. It is built around helping create a culture of missionary discipleship in the Church. We offer a nine-month Parish Partnership that helps you execute on the Four Keys outlined in this book. We also do events aimed at key parts of the culture change journey. Our parish renewal event is called Ascent. This is a kerygmatic parish mission aimed at preaching the Gospel to Catholics and inviting them to respond. Our School of Prayer teaches the fundamentals of the interior life, and our School of Missionary Discipleship does the same for the fundamentals of being a disciple on mission. Our Leadership Summit is an off-site for whoever you want to gather around a table to get aligned with this vision for culture change: this can include parish staff, key leaders, or anyone you feel should be part of enacting this new vision for your parish.

- **M3 Catholic:** Deacon Keith Strohm is one of the greatest missionary discipleship minds in the Church today. Through dynamic events, training, keynotes, and consulting, Deacon Keith helps equip your parish for mission.

- **Catholic Missionary Disciples:** Marcel Lejeune led the charge in building one of the most dynamic and disciple-forming campus ministries in the country, St. Mary's Student Center at Texas A&M. Now he is personally coaching dozens of diocesan and parish leaders through both small 12-week cohorts of other Catholic leaders and one-on-one mentoring in discipleship principles.

- **ID 916:** If you have a heart for reaching Millennials and Gen Z in a particular way, look no further than Renewal Ministries' ID 916. Led by Pete Burak, this group is planting chapters of outreach to these generations in parishes across the country.

OTHER PARISH RENEWAL ORGANIZATIONS WE RECOMMEND

- **Amazing Parish:** Founded by Patrick Lencioni and

John Martin, this inspiring conference with your leadership team is followed by free coaching focused on leading culture change as a team. Their highly trained parish support staff help your team work effectively and support the pastor in his vision.

- **Divine Renovation Network:** The book *Divine Renovation* is one of the best books on parish renewal ever written. Father James Mallon, Ron Huntley, and the rest of the Divine Renovation team now coach parishes through the Divine Renovation Network. They also offer conferences, a great podcast, and other amazing books on parish renewal.

- **FOCUS:** FOCUS (Fellowship of Catholic University Students) has taken their model of spiritual multiplication, which has been so effective on college campuses, and is making it available for parishes.

- **The Evangelical Catholic:** An organization out of Madison, Wisconsin, the Evangelical Catholic does a really good job of building a movement of person-to-person evangelization in parishes. Check them out at evangelicalcatholic.org.

PARISH-BASED DISCIPLEMAKING RESOURCES/PROCESSES/PROGRAMS

- **Alpha:** Alpha is a really good process for initial proclamation and introducing people to the person of Jesus Christ. Alpha is a series of sessions exploring the basics of the Christian faith. Typically run over eleven weeks, each session looks at a different question that people have about faith and is designed to create conversation. It's just an open, informal, and honest space to explore and discuss life's big questions together. Some object to Alpha because it was not originally a Catholic program, but I have seen it used in multiple parishes now and have never encountered any issues.

- **ChristLife:** The ChristLife series is a three-step evangelization process. Discovering Christ, Following Christ, and Sharing Christ are about equipping Catholics for the essential work of evangelization so that all people might personally encounter Jesus Christ and be transformed into his missionary disciples.

- **CCO:** CCO faith-study series are among the best I have encountered for use in small evangelization and discipleship groups. They also now have coaching for building a multiplying movement of discipleship in parishes.

- **Ascension Press:** Some of the Ascension Press video-based Bible studies are quite good and focused on disciplines of discipleship, especially Michael Gormley's series on Community Groups and the Oremus series on a life of prayer.

- **Called and Gifted:** This program from Sherry Weddell's Catherine of Siena Institute helps people discern their specific charisms and how to use them for mission.

APPENDIX 2

Simple and Practical Ideas for Implementing the Four Keys

Remember, the point of this book is not giving you all of the answers for parish renewal, to propose principles for you to wrestle with. However, if you are struggling with beginning to implement the four keys, here are just a couple things you can try to get you started. Culture change is not just about doing a few things differently, it is about applying a radically different lens to how we understand the purpose of our parishes. Still, it can help to have some practical jumping-off points. To that end, here are a few things you might choose to try.

KEY #1: CAST VISION

In working with parishes, I have found that a "missional kick-off weekend" has been a really effective way to begin to cast vision with these core groups. Capital campaigns have used these weekends to great effect. The pastor preaches at all the Masses, sharing the *Why* behind the campaign and hoping to inspire participation and action. If he does not start with *Why*, he risks alienating people and making them resent the campaign. The same kind of weekend can be an effective way

163

of drawing a definitive line in the sand, letting everyone know that this is where the parish is headed.

Just the simple act of announcing the intended cultural shift in a public manner, at every weekend Mass, even if we do not have the journey perfectly plotted out, really helps to set off the process of culture change.

Here are some tips for making the launch weekend a really effective tool:

- Work with a professional graphic designer to craft marketing pieces (new brand and logo, signage, email blasts, bulletin inserts, etc.) that communicate clearly the new mission of the parish to form disciples as well as the clear path to discipleship.

- Precede the launch weekend with a one- or two-day offsite retreat for your core leadership, where you can give them time to wrestle with the call to become a parish of missionary disciples and begin to let them take ownership of how you are going to get there. When we do this for parishes, we use five sessions: 1) The Call of the New Evangelization, 2) Discipleship: Living and Personal Faith, 3) The Process of Conversion: Our Parish's Clear Path to Discipleship, 4) Evangelization Nuts and Bolts, and 5) A Time of Empowerment and Prayer.

- Follow the launch weekend with a town hall meeting one weekday night, giving people time to think of their questions to bring to the meeting.

- Send delegates to communicate and promote the vision to key groups in the parish like Faith Formation Leaders, key ministries, etc.

- Have a follow-up homily series at Sunday and daily Masses communicating more about the *How*: each step in the clear path to discipleship and where it fits in the vision, urging people to begin with a renewed personal encounter with God.

KEY #2: CRAFT A CLEAR PATH
TO DISCIPLESHIP

Really, the best exercise here is to go back through the questions in chapter 5 to build your own parish's clear path to discipleship. Below are some simple ideas for things you can do to start hitting the key parts of the catechumenal model at your parish.

Five Practical Pre-evangelization Ideas

1) Invite everyone in your neighborhood to the parish picnic with fun things to do for kids.

2) Train groups of people to make individual connections with people they do not recognize at Mass.

3) Have a really robust welcoming committee of couples who invite new families and individuals at the parish over for dinner when they register.

4) Incorporate local events to bring awareness to your parish. Have a presence at anything that is a big gathering of people in your parish.

5) Offer ministries that serve your community. Invite others to volunteer with you.

Five Practical Evangelization Ideas

1) Host nights of adoration and worship with dynamic speakers.

2) Bring in a program like Alpha or ChristLife.

3) Teach people to invite their friends to practice person-to-person evangelization using the CCO Discovery series.

4) Train people to give their testimonies.

5) Incorporate the full kerygma in every message you give.

Five Practical Discipleship Ideas
1) Teach people to have a personal prayer life.
2) Host a weekly night of formation with speakers, food, and prayers.
3) Build an adoration chapel and offer more confessions.
4) Build and launch mid-sized community groups (20–40) that have a vision for invitational evangelization built into them by encouraging members to invite people to these groups.
5) Run six-week discipleship groups during Advent and Lent using CCO materials.

Five Practical Apostolate Ideas
1) Do leadership development summits where you train people on the pathway and how to use it.
2) Do an annual ministry formation day where you train anyone who will be involved in leadership.
3) Run Called and Gifted or use the ReLit program from Michael Dopp to train a group in a vision for evangelization.
4) Host an annual parish mission trip either domestically or internationally.
5) Begin building missional communities in your parish where groups discern the practical outreach they are called to.

KEY #3: MOBILIZE LEADERS
(See also, some of the ideas under the Apostolate section above.)

Other things you can start doing to bring other leaders along in this culture change journey are ...

1) Attend an Amazing Parish Conference and get their coaching to build a healthy leadership

team.

2) Have consistent missionary formation for your staff.

3) Have consistent ways to be forming and sending leaders on a quarterly basis.

4) Hang signs around the office and the parish with the mission of the parish and the discipleship pathway.

5) Intentionally raise up at least three other leaders by investing in them at least weekly.

KEY #4: ALIGN EVERYTHING

Marriage Prep

I am increasingly hearing good things about Witness to Love, founded by Ryan and Mary Rose Verret out of Louisiana. You can find out more about them at witnesstolove.org. Witness to Love is a virtues-based, Catechumenate model of marriage renewal and preparation that integrates modern principles of psychology and the virtues to help couples facilitate an authentic dialogue about their relationship.

RCIA

1) Consider using an evangelization process for inquiry.

2) Move to a year-round RCIA model so that you can intake and begin walking with people at any time.

3) Disciple sponsors as they are discipling. Maybe even make RCIA sponsors a set ministry of volunteer disciples at your parish who can walk with others.

4) Do not neglect the full deposit of Faith. Teach salvation history, how to pray, etc.

Religious Education

It seems to me that any religious education model that does not actively attempt to evangelize families is severely lacking. Many are finding more success by moving to a Family Faith

Formation model. A model can only go so far, however; it is all in how you implement it, so good questions to ask would be:

1) How are we building community for parents in our RE program?

2) How are we actively helping parents in our RE program encounter Jesus personally?

The key is to invest in some parents who are already disciples and train them to be a Religious Education core team who have a special interest in evangelizing the other parents. Give them freedom to discern how they can best accomplish the two goals above.

HOW TO MAKE MAJOR LITURGICAL HOLY DAYS IMPACTFUL

Here is a list of things you can do to make major holy days (especially Christmas, Ash Wednesday, and Easter) more missionally impactful:

1) Pray and fast leading up to the day. Pray for the people who will be coming to church at Christmas, Easter, or Ash Wednesday, that their hearts will be moved.

2) Connect the cradle and the cross. Christmas is inherently connected to the Cross. The most powerful Christmas messages I have heard make sure to make the connection to Easter abundantly clear.

3) Have a follow-up. Focus on one thing you would like to invite people back to. We know too well that most are not going to come back the next week to attend Mass. So schedule something

right after a major liturgical holy day and intentionally invite people back to this at each Mass. This event should be an easy on-ramp for anyone, focused on preaching the Gospel and building community.

4) Prepare people to welcome. There is nothing worse than getting snarled at because you took someone's seat at Christmas. In the weeks leading up to Christmas, prepare regular parishioners to be hospitable and welcoming to all of the visitors.

NOTES

1. Kate Taylor, "Only a single Blockbuster remains open in the entire world. Here's what it's like to visit," *Business Insider* online, last modified March 7, 2019, https://www.businessinsider.com/blockbuster-survives-in-bend-oregon-2018-8.
2. "And then there was one: America has just one Blockbuster left," Fox 4 News, last modified July 13, 2018, https://www.fox4now.com/news/national/and-then-here-was-one-america-has-just-one-blockbuster-left.
3. Wayne Friedman, "Could Blockbuster Video Have Been Netflix?" MediaPost, last modified March 27, 2018, https://www.mediapost.com/publications/article/316647/could-blockbuster-video-have-been-netflix.html.
4. "Catholics – Religion in America: US Religious Data, Demographics and Statistics," Pew Research Center, accessed July 5, 2019, https://www.pewforum.org/religious-landscape-study/religious-tradition/catholic/.
5. Jordan Otero Sisson, "Archdiocese Plan Calls For Sweeping Changes For Connecticut Catholics," *Hartford Courant* online, May 7, 2017, https://www.courant.com/news/connecticut/hc-hartford-archdiocese-pastoral-plan-announced-20170506-story.html; Hansi Lo Wang, "'It's All About Church Closings': Catholic Parishes Shrink in Northeast, Midwest," NPR, https://www.npr.org/2015/09/14/436938871/-it-s-all-about-church-closings-catholic-parishes-shrink-in-northeast.
6. "Frequently Requested Church Statistics," Center for

Applied Research in the Apostolate, accessed July 5, 2019, https://cara.georgetown.edu/frequently-requested-church -statistics/.

7. Jack Jenkins, "'Nones' now as big as evangelicals, Catholics in the US," Religion News Service, https://religionnews .com/2019/03/21/nones-now-as-big-as-evangelicals-catholics -in-the-us/.

8. John Paul II, *Redemptoris Missio* (On the permanent validity of the Church's missionary mandate), December 7, 1990, http://w2.vatican.va/content/john-paul-ii/en/encyclicals /documents/hf_jp-ii_enc_07121990_redemptoris -missio.html, §92.

9. "Most Outstanding Personality – 1953," in "5th Emmy Awards Nominees and Winners," Television Academy, Emmys, accessed July 4, 2019, https://www.emmys.com/awards /nominees-winners/1953/most-outstanding-television -personality.

10. John Lennon, quoted in the *London Evening Standard,* March 4, 1966, http://www.beatlesinterviews.org /db1966.0304-beatles-john-lennon-were-more-popular-than -jesus-now-maureen-cleave.html.

11. "Frequently Requested Church Statistics," CARA, accessed July 8, 2019, https://cara.georgetown.edu /frequently-requested-church-statistics/.

12. Josh Scherer, "In-N-Out Drive Thru Lines Are a Public Menace, and Here's How They Can Be Stopped," *Los Angeles Magazine* online, September 30, 2016, https://www.lamag .com/digestblog/n-drive-thru-lines-public-menace -heres-can-stopped/.

13. Saint John of the Cross, quoted in *John of the Cross: Selected Writings,* ed. Kieran Kavanaugh and Ernest E. Larkin (Mahwah, NJ: Paulist Press, 1988), 270.

14. George Weigel, *Evangelical Catholicism: Deep Reform in the 21st-Century Church* (New York: Basic Books, 2013), 92–93.

15. Katie Galioto, "Chicago Catholics struggle to build future with fewer priests as parishes shrink, cash dwindles," *Chicago Tribune* online, January 4, 2019, https://www.chicagotribune.com/news/breaking/ct-met-chicago-catholic-church-20181228-story.html.

16. Sabrina Arena Ferrisi, "Vocations in America," *Legatus Magazine* online, last modified December 1, 2009, https://legatus.org/vocations-in-america/.

17. John Paul II, *Ecclesia in America,* Vatican website, January 22, 1999, http://w2.vatican.va/content/john-paul-ii/en/apost_exhortations/documents/hf_jp-ii_exh_22011999_ecclesia-in-america.html, §73.

18. Deacon Greg Kandra, "A flood of vocations from one parish in Michigan," Beliefnet, accessed July 5, 2019, https://www.beliefnet.com/columnists/deacons-bench/2007/09/a-flood-of-vocations-from-one-parish-in-michigan.html.

19. Paul VI, *Evangelii Nuntiandi,* Vatican website, October 8, 1975, http://w2.vatican.va/content/paul-vi/en/apost_exhortations/documents/hf_p-vi_exh_19751208_evangelii-nuntiandi.html, §14.

20. Ibid., §18.

21. Aristotle, *Nicomachean Ethics,* Book 2.

22. John Paul II, 15th World Youth Day: Address of the Holy Father John Paul II — Vigil of Prayer, Vatican website, August 19, 2000, http://w2.vatican.va/content/john-paul-ii/en/speeches/2000/jul-sep/documents/hf_jp-ii_spe_20000819_gmg-veglia.html.

23. Saint Athanasius, *De Incarnatione Verbi Dei* 54, 3: PG 25, 192B.

24. Benedict XVI, *Deus Caritas Est,* Vatican website, December 25, 2005, http://w2.vatican.va/content/benedict-xvi/en/encyclicals/documents/hf_ben-xvi_enc_20051225_deus-caritas-est.html, §1.

25. "When Americans Say They Believe in God, What Do

They Mean?" Pew Research Center, Religion & Public Life, April 25, 2018, https://www.pewforum.org/2018/04/25/when -americans-say-they-believe-in-god-what-do-they-mean/.

26. Benedict XVI, *Verbum Domini*, Vatican website, September 30, 2010, http://w2.vatican.va/content/benedict-xvi/en /apost_exhortations/documents/hf_ben-xvi_exh_20100930 _verbum-domini.html, §25.

27. John Paul II, *Ecclesia in America*, §73.

28. John Paul II, *Redemptoris Missio*, §46.

29. Steve Jobs, "Think different/Crazy ones," September 23, 1997, https://www.youtube.com/watch?v=keCwRdbwNQY.

30. Simon Sinek, *Start with Why*, 227

31. Patrick Vlaskovits, "Henry Ford, Innovation, and That 'Faster Horse' Quote," *Harvard Business Review* online, August 29, 2011, https://hbr.org/2011/08/henry-ford-never -said-the-fast.

32. Simon Sinek, "How great leaders inspire action," TED Conference online videos, accessed July 5, 2019, https://www.ted.com/talks/simon_sinek_how_great_leaders _inspire_action?language=en.

33. Josef Pieper, *Leisure: The Basis of Culture* (South Bend, IN: St. Augustine's Press, 1998), 48.

34. Congregation for the Clergy, *General Directory for Catechesis*, §90.

35. Jerry Bruckheimer, *Remember the Titans,* DVD, directed by Boaz Yakin (Burbank, CA: Buena Vista Pictures, 2000).

36. Saint Ignatius of Loyola, "Rules for the Same Effect with Greater Discernment of Spirits," in Spiritual Exercises, Internet Sacred Text Archive, accessed July 5, 2019, https://www .sacred-texts.com/chr/seil/seil79.htm.

37. Georges Lemaître, "Contributions to a British Association Discussion on the Evolution of the Universe," Nature 128 (October 1931): 704–706, doi: 10.1038/128704a0.

38. John Paul II, Ad Limina Visit of the Bishops of Southern Germany, December 4, 1992, quoted in A. Dulles, *John Paul*

II and the New Evangelization: What Does It Mean?, ed. R. Martin and P. Williamson (Cincinnati: Servant, 2006), 13.

39. John Paul II, *Redemptoris Missio*, §44.

40. John Paul II, *Catechesi Tradendae*, Vatican website, October 16, 1979, http://w2.vatican.va/content/john-paul-ii/en /apost_exhortations/documents/hf_jp-ii_exh_16101979 _catechesi-tradendae.html, §25.

41. Will Mancini, "How to Measure Real Church Growth," accessed July 8, 2019, https://www.willmancini.com/blog /how-to-measure-real-church-growth.

42. Benedict XVI, Inaugural Session of the Fifth General Conference of the Bishops of Latin America and the Caribbean: Address of His Holiness Benedict XVI, Vatican website, May 13, 2007, http://w2.vatican.va/content/benedict-xvi/en /homilies/2007/documents/hf_ben-xvi_hom_20070513 _conference-brazil.html, §3.

43. John Paul II, *Christifideles Laici*, Vatican website, December 30, 1988, http://w2.vatican.va/content/john-paul-ii/en /apost_exhortations/documents/hf_jp-ii_exh_30121988 _christifideles-laici.html, §23; "Laity Must Not Be Clericalized Nor Clergy Laicized, Says Pope," ZENIT, last modified May 9, 2002, https://zenit.org/articles/laity-must-not-be -clericalized-nor-clergy-laicized-says-pope/.

44. Roger Landry, "Pope Francis and the Reform of the Laity," *National Catholic Register* online, April 11, 2013, http://www.ncregister.com/daily-news/pope-francis-and-the -reform-of-the-laity.

45. Michael Lipka, "The number of U.S. Catholics has grown, so why are there fewer parishes?" Pew Research Center, last modified November 6, 2014, https://www.pewresearch .org/fact-tank/2014/11/06/the-number-of-u-s-catholics-has -grown-so-why-are-there-fewer-parishes/.

46. Lydia Saad, "Catholics' Church Attendance Resumes Downward Slide," Gallup, last modified April 9, 2018, https://news.gallup.com/poll/232226/church

-attendance-among-catholics-resumes-downward-slide.aspx.

47. Scott Thumma and Warren Bird, "Recent Shifts in America's Largest Protestant Churches: Megachurches 2015 Report," Leadership Network & Hartford Institute, http://hirr.hartsem.edu/megachurch/2015_Megachurches _Report.pdf (p. 2).

48. Mother Teresa, "Letter of the Foundress," quoted in John Paul II, "Letter on the 50th Anniversary of the Missionaries of Charity," Vatican website, October 2, 2000, http://w2.vatican.va /content/john-paul-ii/en/letters/2000/documents/hf_jp-ii _let_20001017_missionaries-charity.html.

49. "Jesus sent by the Father for the salvation of the world," Vatican website, accessed July 5, 2019, http://www.vatican.va /jubilee_2000/magazine/documents/ju_mag_01041998 _p-24_en.html.

50. Archbishop Vigneron, "Unleash the Gospel," UTG, June 3, 2017, https://www.unleashthegospel.org/the-letter/ (part 5).

51. Robert J. McCarty and John M. Vitek, *Going, Going, Gone: The Dynamics of Disaffiliation in Young Catholics* (Winona, MN:Saint Mary's Press, 2018).

52. Christopher White, "New study seeks to understand why young people leave the Church," Crux, last modified January 17, 2018, https://cruxnow.com/church-in-the-usa/2018/01/17 /new-study-seeks-understand-young-people-leave-church/.

53. Ryan Erskine, "20 Online Reputation Statistics That Every Business Owner Needs To Know," *Forbes* online, last modified September 19, 2017, https://www.forbes.com/sites /ryanerskine/2017/09/19/20-online-reputation -statistics-that-every-business-owner-needs-to-know /#1cf0650acc5c.

54. "The State of Influencer Marketing 2019: Benchmark Report [+Infographic]," Influencer Marketing Hub, last modified May 28, 2019, https://influencermarketinghub.com /influencer-marketing-2019-benchmark-report/.

55. "The Most Post-Christian Cities in America: 2019," Barna

Group, last modified June 5, 2019, https://www.barna.com
/research/post-christian-cities-2019/.
56. Pope Benedict XVI, *Faith and the Future* (San Francisco,
CA: Ignatius Press, 2009).
57. Phyllis Tickle, *The Great Emergence: How Christianity Is
Changing and Why* (Grand Rapids, MI: Baker Books, 2012).
58. Friedrich Nietzsche, *The Gay Science*, trans. Walter
Kaufmann (New York: Vintage Books, 1974), 181.

ABOUT THE AUTHOR

Tim Glemkowski is the president and founder of L'Alto Catholic Institute, a not-for-profit apostolate dedicated to helping parishes become more effective at forming disciples. Tim is a sought-after international speaker and leader who has served in various roles in evangelization including teaching high school theology, youth and young adult ministry at a parish, and as a director of evangelization and catechesis. He double-majored in theology and philosophy at Franciscan University of Steubenville and has his Master's in Theology from the Augustine Institute in Denver, Colorado. Tim is passionate about seeing the Church renewed through discipleship. You can often find him hiking in the Rockies with his wife, Maggie, and their children.

You Might Also Like

Forming Intentional Disciples: The Path to Knowing and Following Jesus
By Sherry A. Weddell

These are times of immense challenge and immense opportunity for the Catholic Church:

- Only 30 percent of Americans who were raised Catholic are still practicing.
- Fully 10 percent of all adults in America are ex-Catholics.
- Only 60 percent of Catholics believe in a personal God.

If the Church is to reverse these trends, the evangelizers must first be evangelized. In other words, Catholics-in-the-pew must make

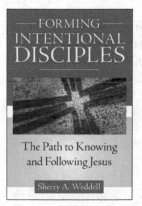

a conscious choice to know and follow Jesus before they can draw others to him. This work of discipleship lies at the heart of **Forming Intentional Disciples**, a book designed to help Church leaders, parish staff and all Catholics transform parish life from within.

Learn about the five thresholds of postmodern conversion, how to open a conversation about faith and belief, how to ask thought-provoking questions and establish an atmosphere of trust, when to tell the Great Story of Jesus, how to help someone respond to God's call to intentional discipleship, and much more.

Also available in Spanish. Companion study guide also available.

You Might Also Like

Becoming a Parish of Intentional Disciples

In her first book, **Forming Intentional Disciples: The Path to Knowing and Following Jesus**, Sherry A. Weddell captured the attention of Catholics across the globe as she uncovered the life-changing power that accompanies the conscious decision to follow Jesus as his disciple.

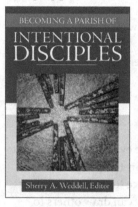

Now, in the groundbreaking **Becoming a Parish of Intentional Disciples**, she has gathered experienced leaders and collaborators whose exceptional field-tested wisdom and enthusiasm for transforming Catholic parishes into centers of discipleship and apostolic outreach is both inspiring and practical.

As Sherry asks in her own chapter, "Are we willing to answer the call and pay the price necessary to become a new generation of saints through which God can do extraordinary things in our time?"

You Might Also Like

Fruitful Discipleship: Living the Mission of Jesus in the Church and the World
By Sherry A. Weddell

"By this my Father is glorified, that you bear much fruit, and so prove to be my disciples." — John 15:8

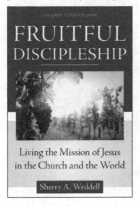

How does God's grace change our individual lives, families, neighborhoods, parish communities, and cities? In **Fruitful Discipleship**, Sherry A. Weddell describes how the Holy Spirit is at work in all the baptized—calling and gifting us to "say yes" in ways that will be the longed-for answer to someone else's prayers and fuel the mission of the whole Church. God has chosen to be present in this world through the faith and obedience of missionary disciples who witness to Jesus Christ and bear abundant fruit. In **Fruitful Discipleship**, Sherry:

- identifies and explains 23 distinct charisms
- provides wise guidance for discerning and exercising the gifts received in baptism
- sheds light on the implications of those gifts for both service and leadership
- encourages readers with true stories of parishes, cities, and dioceses that are experiencing powerful renewal